JOURNEY
TO UNDERSTANDING

Equipping Christians to
Engage Muslims *with Faith*

JOURNEY
TO UNDERSTANDING

Equipping Christians to
Engage Muslims *with Faith*

GLOBAL INITIATIVE
REACHING **MUSLIM** PEOPLES

Journey to Understanding
Equipping Christians to Engage Muslims with Faith
By Global Initiative: Reaching **Muslim** Peoples

Printed in the United States of America
ISBN: 1-880689-37-5
Copyright 2018, Global Initiative

Published by Onward Books, Inc., Springfield, MO

Cover Design and Interior Layout by Tony Scheibelhut

DEDICATION

This book is dedicated to the faithful believers around the world who have embraced the opportunity, regardless of the challenge, to engage Muslims with the gospel. Their example made the testimonies of salvation included within this book possible.

TABLE OF CONTENTS

Foreword   Doug Clay 9

Introduction 13

Lessons:

   1. Our Attitude and God's Love 21

   2. Compelled by Lostness 43

   3. Holy Spirit Empowerment for 75
      Proclaiming the Gospel

   4. Outreach to Muslims: Creating a 111
      New Environment

   5. Developing Christians from a 145
      Muslim Background

Endnotes 181

Addendum 183

About the Authors 189

FOREWORD

I am deeply grateful to Global Initiative: Reaching Muslim Peoples for creating *Journey to Understanding*, a powerful resource that teaches Christians to understand Muslims and engage them with the message of Jesus.

There are 1.6 billion Muslims in the world. An estimated 4.5 to 6 million Muslims live in America. Thousands more arrive annually, mostly from restricted-access countries where they have never heard an adequate presentation of Jesus. *Journey to Understanding* teaches that equipped believers and local churches are the essential ingredients in reaching the growing Muslim community.

The underpinning premise of *Journey to Understanding* is the importance of intercessory prayer. Practicing Muslims are obligated to pray 5 times a day. By the age of 70, a Muslim will hear the "call to prayer" 127,750 times! This book goes to the spiritual heart of the matter: that any effective outreach to Muslims will be the outcome of sustained intercessory prayer. Ultimately, it is spiritual power encounter through intercessory prayer that successfully counters the spiritual vacuum of Islam.

Journey to Understanding awakened me to the importance of reflecting the love of God in my attitude toward Muslims. The very nature of the Father is love; thus our attitude toward Muslims must clearly reflect His loving nature. A reminder of this truth is found in Romans 5:8: "But God shows his love for us in that while we were still sinners, Christ died for us."

This timely book is filled with biblical insight and observations to help you understand Muslims. But more than that, it is written to give you a scriptural framework that will equip you to share the truth about Jesus with Muslims. The structure of the book facilitates easy reading while providing very teachable material. I highly recommend it for individuals, churches and constituencies.

—Doug Clay
General Superintendent of the Assemblies of God

ACKNOWLEDGMENTS

The authors express their deepest appreciation to Ken and Peggy Horn of Onward Books. Their prayers, patience and professional guidance are reflected throughout this resource.

INTRODUCTION:
OUR MOTIVATION AS CHRISTIANS

With the final days of this age approaching, there are still far too many people lacking the most important information of all—the truth about God and His Son, Jesus. This crucial knowledge impacts the most important issue of life: eternity—and where each person will spend it.

She's Muslim, I thought as my eyes caught sight of the veiled woman in line ahead of me. *Probably an immigrant.*

But when I heard her speak to the checkout lady, I realized that she had a very distinct American accent. And when I got a better look at her, I saw she had blue eyes and wisps of blonde hair had escaped her veil.

Marcia was raised in a Christian home and had accepted Christ as her Savior at an early age. In her early 20s, she had married a "born-again" believer who turned out to be very abusive. After their divorce, a bitter Marcia blamed God for the situation.

In a backslidden condition, Marcia went to work at a hospital. She clearly remembers the day she met "the man of her dreams."

"It was just before noon and I was standing by the nurse's station when my thoughts were interrupted by a voice telling the charge nurse he needed to take a few minutes off for noon prayer. When I looked up, the man who spoke was just a few feet away. He had an accent and his mannerisms were rather different. Though I had been a Christian all my life, I had never known anyone who asked for prayer time, so his request impressed me a great deal.

"For the next few weeks he was assigned to me for training. As we worked together I really enjoyed his good sense of humor and his charming manners. Not once did I hear him use profanity or show disrespect to anyone. He was working to support his education plans, and had great love for the elderly. He always took time to listen to them. I could tell he was from a good, close and loving family with a high sense of moral values.

"As time passed, I found myself drawn to his piercing dark brown eyes, mannerisms, and the way he called my name. He was an attractive man who believed in family and his religion, and he had a great sense of morality. I was so attracted to him I didn't even take time to learn more about Islam. He fit the profile of a good, godly man that my parents had always tried to paint in my mind. He never smoked, drank or cursed. He was pro-life and anti-divorce and always said, 'god willing (*Insha-Allah*).'

"Before we could enter a deeper relationship, he insisted on meeting my family, which lived some 150 miles away. This concept alone impressed me a great deal.

"After he met my parents, he contacted his family to give them his good report and we proceeded with our plans to be married. When I suggested a church, we had our first disagreement. It was impossible for his family from the Middle East to attend a church so we compromised and had a private wedding ceremony.

"During the first few months of our marriage we had several discussions about religion which ended in heated arguments. Thus, we decided not to bring up the subject of Jesus as the Son of God, and the crucifixion story. I was allowed to go to church Christmas, Easter and Mother's Day. But on the way home we would engage in terrible arguments. He would say that I shamed him and the honor of his family because I wouldn't submit to Islam.

"Except for our religious differences, our life was going well until the birth of our first son. I had never seen any man happier to have a son than my husband. He called his family the day our son was born and they were all proud of us. They praised me highly. My husband said that he was proud of me and that Allah, too, was pleased with me. For a short time I was the jewel on the family crown and it felt wonderful. I was proud to be his wife and the mother of our son.

"After the birth of our first son, my husband became more zealous in his faith. He declared our son was a Muslim and by Islamic law I was a Muslim through marriage. Our son was given an Islamic name and I was informed that my husband had already whispered verses from the Quran in his ear after birth.

"Mixed feelings of anger and resentment came over me. How could he deceive me like this? He had changed and I felt as if I didn't know him anymore. All he could think about was to raise his son as a Muslim. We fought and raised our voices in anger almost every day. He was trying to isolate me from everyone, including my family, and though he never raised his hand to me, I wondered when that would happen.

"I became very depressed and thoughts of suicide flooded my mind. How could this beautiful, loving, caring man change to such a terrifying nightmare? What did I do and where did I go wrong? I just wanted to lie down, go to sleep and never wake up again.

"Two years later we had our second son. By this time I was not allowed to go to church at all and our second son was called Muhammad. Years passed and because of my pride I was afraid to confide in my parents about my self-made situation. What I once loved about this Muslim man, I now hated. He mentioned many times that a divorce was not an option. He said he would take my sons and disappear in his country and I would never see them again.

"I began to pray to the Lord to somehow relieve me and my sons from such a heavy burden. I prayed and read my hidden Bible, and finally decided to visit a church without his knowledge. The Lord restored my lost relationship with Him and His Word gave me strength to walk one step at a time. He also restored my relationship with my parents who had been praying and seeking God's face on my behalf. Many churches were interceding for my family and me. I lived my life daily as the Bible directed me and as a Christian wife should and my husband's treatment of me began to improve.

"After a while he did not object to me reading my Bible and going to church. He even visited the church I attended on occasion. Whenever he would argue about the deity of Christ, I just kept my peace and prayed.

"I prayed and fasted for the salvation of my husband. And though our life was still up and down, I was determined to serve the Lord no matter what.

"The Lord began to open my husband's eyes to see some miracles of healing in my father's life. As the result of ongoing prayers by hundreds of partners in the Lord, and unconditional love, my husband began reading the Bible. By the power of the Holy Spirit and grace of God, my husband became fascinated with the story of Jesus. He was drawn to the Fisher of Men, and Jesus manifested himself to my husband in such a powerful way that eventually he was not only saved, but also baptized in the Holy Spirit."

Our desire at Global Initiative: Reaching Muslim Peoples is to be part of others' stories who have had their eternal destiny changed because we have changed. Our desire is for you to be equipped—in mind and spirit—to share the knowledge of Jesus with Muslim people wherever you encounter them.

In America, most people have opportunities to hear God's truth. But what about America's Muslims? Do they ever hear about Christ and His love for them? In the past 36 years the number of Muslims worldwide has more than doubled to 1.6 billion.

In America there are an estimated 4.5 to 6 million Muslims, who may be among our coworkers, fellow students, or even our neighbors. The three largest ethnic groups of Muslims in America are Southeast Asians, African-Americans, and those from the Middle East. These coworkers, fellow students and neighbors are further distinguished by the particular sect of Islam that they follow. These include Sunni, Shia, Sufi, Ahmadiyya, the Nation of Islam, and other minority groups. For them, God's truth is still very much hidden even though they live among followers of Jesus.

Many Muslims in America are descendants of immigrants who arrived from countries where the preaching of the gospel is limited. In these areas the gospel has been intentionally restricted or Christians have been reluctant to share their faith. God has commissioned His Church to be a part of the process of leading the Muslims who now call America their home to a correct understanding of Jesus.

We want to help you understand the basic beliefs and practices that facilitate conversation. But we don't want you to feel you must become an expert in Islam to be a witness. The qualities that will attract Muslims are a loving attitude, devotion to God, and a sincere interest in them—not just our knowledge. In fact, dialogue concerning their faith creates an atmosphere of respect for them as individuals.

As a follower of Jesus Christ, we should view Muslims as people in need. Our prayer is that you would so influence your Muslim friends that they would seek out Jesus. This is the pattern we encounter in the Gospel of John. The first recorded words of Jesus to the future disciple Andrew were, "What are you seeking?" (1:38). Andrew wanted to know where Jesus was staying so he could join Him. Jesus said, "Come and you will see." Andrew wanted relationship. Jesus' last exhortation was given to Peter. "Follow me" (21:19), He said. Jesus called Peter to obedience and faith. We want Muslims to respond to Jesus by receiving Him and the love He has for them.

Where do we begin? Throughout this book you will find an emphasis on prayer. Islam teaches that no one should be outside the sound of the call to prayer. The obligation to pray five times a day is one of the five major religious duties of

Islam. It is not a suggestion or an option; it is mandatory. By the age of 70, a Muslim will have been "called to pray" at least 127,750 times. What about us? Have we heard a "Call to Prayer"?

"When he saw the crowds, he had compassion for them, because they were harassed and helpless, like sheep without a shepherd. Then he said to his disciples, 'The harvest is plentiful, but the laborers are few; therefore pray earnestly to the Lord of the harvest to send out laborers into his harvest'" (Matthew 9:36-38).

The Holy Spirit will help us to focus our attention on intercessory prayer. We are reminded daily that we are wrestling not against flesh and blood, but against principalities, powers and rulers of darkness. The result we seek—to see all Muslims receive an adequate witness of the truth about Jesus Christ and the opportunity to accept Him as Savior—will come only with groanings of spiritual intercession. There just is no substitute. There is no "easier solution." This is where we begin! Prayer is not only where we begin, but continual prayer will keep us focused on the task. (See addendum for additional direction on prayer.)

As you begin this journey, a second question will set the stage for what is to follow: "Where am I?" This book, you will quickly discover, endeavors to take its readers to the place God desires them to be in His service—engaging Muslims. As you go through the five chapters, it is our prayer that you will see the challenge the Church encounters when dealing with Islam. Let your sight rise above the difficulties and seize each challenge as your opportunity.

OUR ATTITUDE AND GOD'S LOVE

The objective for Lesson 1 is:

To develop a godly love for Muslims.

CHAPTER SUMMARY

In this lesson we will discuss the biblical attitude toward the lost and how it relates to Muslim people. We will address how the "church" views Muslims in America and evaluate that view from a biblical perspective, especially examining God's desire "not wishing that any should perish" (2 Peter 3:9).

Testimony of a Former Muslim

"When I thought about Allah, I did not see him as a wonderful God, loving and caring for all people ... but as this big giant guy who was going to crush me. I couldn't see myself going to heaven, according to the Quran and all that teaching. I couldn't weigh my good deeds against my bad deeds and see myself winning.... I asked myself, *Where is God now?*"

A Christian woman gave this man a cassette tape, which he listened to in his car. His response: "The man speaking in that cassette tape ... I felt him speaking directly to me. He asked, 'You want the love of God, don't you?' And I just started weeping. I said, 'Yes, I want that love of God. I need that love of God.... If I know that this God whom I believe in will wash all my sins away, then I'm glad to be His servant.'"

CHAPTER OUTLINE

Present Environment

Drawn by Love

How Does the Church View Muslims in America?

Evaluating the Attitude of the Church

Our Attitudes and Priorities

Testimony

Biblical Examples of Unchristlike Attitudes Toward the Lost

Jesus in the Temple

Jonah and the People of Nineveh

Biblical Examples of a Transformed Attitude for the Lost

James and John, and a Samaritan Village

Peter at the House of Cornelius

Conclusion

Prayer Points

Action Steps

Review Questions

PRESENT ENVIRONMENT

Drawn by Love

Before focusing on Muslims or any person who is lost without Christ, we first must consider our own spiritual condition. To really love the lost requires a burning passion for Jesus. From the common fisherman, tax collector, or religious radical, to the highly educated Pharisee, Jesus called them all to be with Him. Paul captures this in Romans 12, verses 1-20 (ISV).

In verse one he says, "in view of God's mercies." God has loved us from the beginning of time and that love will never change. Paul challenges us to give our lives as "living sacrifices" for His purposes. In verses 9-20, Paul addresses the kind of love we should have toward this lost world. He describes the kind of supernatural love that comes in response to what Jesus has done for us (vv. 9-13). These verses deal with relationships in the family of God. Beginning in verse 14, he describes this love in relationship to those outside of God's family. This would include the Muslims of our day. Yes, God will have the last word when it comes to justice over evil, but until then, we overcome evil by doing good to all men and women including the foreigner. Jesus said it this way: "If anyone would come after me, let him deny himself and take up his cross and follow me" (Mark 8:34). Taking up our cross helps destroy the old nature focused on "me" and my desires. Only by serving and ministering to those who are still in darkness will we experience God's perfect will for our lives.

Today most Muslims in America are seeking something that, for some, did not exist in their land of ancestry. Perhaps they seek freedom, education, healthcare, or peace. However, unknown to them, God has a different plan—freedom from the power of sin and guilt and an experience with God personally through Jesus. God's promise is that all ethnic groups on earth will hear about Jesus before He returns to take His Church (Matthew 24:14).

Earlier we mentioned the numerous sects of Islam. Many members of these sects are not foreign born or immigrants; they are African-Americans. These comprise almost one-third of the Muslims in America. Although the Nation of Islam's roll call numbers a steady twenty thousand, evidence suggests it is far more influential than that number indicates. Although many of the estimated two million African-American Muslims got their start due to the "Nation's" influence, the majority now belong to "orthodox" groups. Carl Ellis, Director of Project Joseph, states:

> The lion's share of those (African-Americans) who are seeking God continue to move toward the mosque. This is ironic because the Bible more adequately addresses African-American concerns than does the Quran. Today's Islamic growth in the United States owes more to the weakness and retreat of the church than it does to the strength and veracity of Islam.[1]

How Does the Church View Muslims in America?

A revealing survey, conducted by the Barna Group, recently found:

- Evangelical Christians have the most unfavorable perception of Islam, 62%

- Protestant clergy expressed a negative attitude toward Islam, 72%

- More than one in four Americans associate Islam with violence, 26%

- Three-quarters of evangelicals believe that Islam is anti-Christian, 74%

In light of current views expressed by the Barna Group poll, it is important that Christians discern between Islam as a religious system, and Muslims as human beings for whom Christ died. Other surveys inform us that Christians are either unaware—or sometimes willfully blinded—of ways they can effectively engage those of the Islamic faith. Simply interpreted, believers' lack of understanding inhibits their witness to Muslims! Most have a concern for Muslims, yet don't know how to begin a conversation. For the most part, they have been hesitant to engage them.

The question should not be, "What is our opinion of Muslims?" but rather, "How does God see the lost?" What words or phrases come to your mind when you hear the word "Muslim"? Popular answers are based on stereotypes. These include: "terrorist," "angry men," "proud," "fear"; "their women are covered, beaten, and abused." Most of us probably identify with one or more of these. But Christians must look deeper. What's required is a **Christian response**, not just a Western cultural one. A true Christian response would include words like: "lost," "seeking," and "blinded by the god of this world" (2 Corinthians 4:4).

Yes, some Muslim countries can be viewed as enemies of America, Israel, and our Christian faith and way of life. But **our responsibility has to do with reaching lost people** not battling hostile governments or cultures! At a time when even believers are tempted to fear or show indifference toward Muslims, Christ followers should be active in demonstrating the gospel with godly attitudes and deeds of love.

EVALUATING THE ATTITUDE OF THE CHURCH

Our Attitudes and Priorities

The thought of witnessing to Muslims commonly leads to a sense of inadequacy. We don't understand their religion, their culture, or worldview. An even more serious problem is that we are just too busy with our own world to be concerned with the world of a Muslim. Permeating attitudes of fear or lack of understanding, accompanied by major differences in culture and language, keep us from inviting Muslims to know Jesus. Our objective is to see these attitudes replaced with concern for their souls, mercy, and the compelling love of the Savior.

Seeking to have the passion of Jesus for Muslims is less daunting when we realize the Holy Spirit is available to supply us with needed strength and direction. Muslims don't come to faith in Christ because of our clever doctrinal arguments. The primary way God uses believers today is by demonstrating the love of Jesus. We must demonstrate that love—by word and deed—to Muslims who are near us.

In spite of all the Christian neglect and all the difficulties we've discussed, there are more Muslims currently coming to faith in Christ than ever before.

Testimony

Emma is 81 years old and lives in Oregon. Recently she went shopping at a warehouse store. As she turned down an aisle, her eyes were drawn to a woman who was veiled in black from head to toe. The woman had a small child with her. Emma, whose close walk with God had familiarized her with the unmistakable voice of the Holy Spirit, now heard Him speak: *Emma, that woman wants to know about Jesus.* She approached the Muslim woman from behind and very gently tapped her on the shoulder. It startled her, but Emma's gentle smile set her at ease. "Hello," Emma began. "Do you want to know about Jesus?"

The Muslim woman looked at her and without hesitancy responded: "Yes, I do. Please tell me." Emma shared while her new friend heard about Jesus for the first time.

BIBLICAL EXAMPLES OF UNCHRISTLIKE ATTITUDES TOWARD THE LOST

Jesus in the Temple

Why do we see so few Muslims coming to our churches? Could it be that Muslims are unwelcomed and lost to the kingdom partly because of the barriers that stand between us? Jesus faced a similar problem in His day. We read about it in Mark 11:15, 17 (NIV): "On reaching Jerusalem, Jesus entered the temple courts and began driving out those who were buying and selling there…. He said, 'Is it not written: 'My house will be called a house of prayer for all nations'?'"

Why was Jesus passionate about what went on in the Temple—the church of His day? The setting is the "Court of the Gentiles" … and it was filled with animals ready to be purchased for Jewish ritual sacrifice. God had said that the Temple was to be "a house of prayer *for all nations*," but its leaders had used it instead to gain wealth and exercise power over God's people. The mission that the Father had sent Jesus to earth to complete was directly impacted by what occurred here.

This was not the plan God had for His Temple. Non-Jews could not have prayed there even if they had wanted to. The Jews called all such foreign peoples "Gentiles"—their word for "outsiders." The heart of Jesus was to make room for those outside His Father's house, outside the family of Israel, and outside the kingdom of God. Jesus' actions teach us that we should seek to build biblical bridges and remove barriers that hinder a proper understanding of God's love.

Jonah and the People of Nineveh

The story of Jonah provides one of the clearest contrasts between a God who is full of compassion for the lost and a servant of God who is unnecessarily full of contempt for the lost. God had commissioned Jonah to go to Nineveh—Israel's archenemy—to preach a message of warning. God was ready to destroy the city for its wickedness. His directive to Jonah was clear: go and preach. But Jonah had other ideas. We can imagine him thinking to himself, *There's no way I'm going to Nineveh. God, don't you remember how they terrorize their adversaries and torment their captives?* So instead of packing for Nineveh, Jonah decides to go on vacation, on a cruise to Tarshish. That's when God uses a storm and a huge fish to change Jonah's mind and direction.

Jonah finally ends up in Nineveh where he does indeed preach God's message. What a powerful sermon it must have been! Not only do the Ninevites repent, but their king declares a city-wide fast. As a result, God responds in mercy and spares the city and its 120,000 inhabitants. This is one of the greatest acts of mercy recorded in all of the Bible. We would expect Jonah to be overwhelmed with joy. But not so! Instead, Jonah is displeased and angry. He knows that if the people repent, God will respond in mercy and compassion—and he wants no part of that scenario. He doesn't want God to save the Ninevites; he wants God to punish them.

Jonah may be a prophet of God, but there is clearly something wrong with this picture. Jonah eventually does all the right things: he goes to the right place; he says the right words; and he preaches with conviction. But in all that he does, there is something tragically missing. **He really does not have a genuine burden for the Ninevites.** There is no pity, compassion, or love.

Today, because of bloody conflicts and persecution in the Middle East, it's as though Islam has become our present-day Nineveh. Like Jonah, some Christians are determined to remain distant from Muslims, and when they do reach out, it is with a message of condemnation and divine retribution—a message void of love and compassion.

It was a Sunday night. The missionary speaker was

walking down the aisle. Many had gathered with the missionary to pray for the salvation of Muslims. As he walked, he was joined by a retired, hardened Marine. The veteran said, "Why don't we nuke them all?" The missionary stopped in dismay. The veteran quickly smiled and said, "I'm just kidding ... but it would be easy."

Some believers actually feel this way. Remove the problem rather than accept the challenge by seizing the opportunity.

The Book of Jonah is the only book of the Bible that ends in a question. The question is very significant because God is the one who poses it. He queries Jonah: "Should not I pity Nineveh?" (Jonah 4:11). The question is never answered. It's as though the Holy Spirit is leaving the question for us to answer in our own context. Of course God should have pity because God is love. But this leads to another critical question: If God has pity, should we not also have pity for the lost? Should we not also be concerned? Of course the answer is yes, and it must apply to Muslim people as well as to everyone else. But for that to happen, we need a change in attitude. Change, from a hardened heart like that of Jonah, to the heart of God who is "not wishing that any should perish, but that all should reach repentance" (2 Peter 3:9).

BIBLICAL EXAMPLES OF A TRANSFORMED ATTITUDE FOR THE LOST

James and John, and a Samaritan Village

Jesus called James and John "the Sons of Thunder" (Mark 3:17). Let's consider their action in Luke 9:51-56. Toward the end of His ministry, as Jesus leads His disciples on one more trip to Jerusalem, they need to spend a night in a Samaritan village. Even though Jews and Samaritans held bitter feelings toward each other, Jesus sends messengers ahead into the village to make lodging arrangements. When word comes back that the Samaritans refuse them hospitality, James and

John explode in anger! "Lord," they ask, "do you want us to tell fire to come down from heaven and consume them?" They are ready to destroy the Samaritans completely! However, Jesus responds with words of rebuke, not at the Samaritans, but at His own disciples. Although John is a close disciple, he too fails to understand the breadth of God's mercy for the lost.

Sad to say, there are still isolated followers of Jesus who would like to call fire down from heaven on the people of Islam. It's true that there are areas in the world where Christians are persecuted by Muslims and churches burned to the ground, believers murdered. It's human nature to want to strike back. But we must keep in mind that most Muslims don't fall under the category of radical militants. Many of them are sincere and hospitable people who have concerns for godliness, modesty, and family values. Furthermore, the Scriptures remind us that we followers of Jesus are to rise above our human nature.

We are no longer to conform to the mindset of the world. Instead, we are to have the mind of Christ and be conformed to His image—the very one who looked down from the cross upon His persecutors and cried out, "Father, forgive them!" We must be careful to demonstrate a Christlike attitude to everyone, including the Muslim people. Remember, "For God so loved the *world*." We cannot exclude anyone.

The fact that God's love is for everyone was confirmed by a wonderful occurrence in a most unlikely place after Christ's resurrection. It all began when persecution broke out against the believers in Jerusalem and scattered them to neighboring regions. According to Acts 8:4-8:

> Now those who were scattered went about preaching the word. Philip went down to the city of Samaria and proclaimed to them the Christ. And the crowds with one accord paid attention to what was being said by

Philip, when they heard him and saw the signs that he did. For unclean spirits, crying out with a loud voice, came out of many who had them, and many who were paralyzed or lame were healed. So there was much joy in that city.

From this description, it is obvious that God was blessing people in a marvelous way. The city was experiencing "much joy." But these were people of Samaria! God was blessing the despised Samaritans. When this news reaches Jerusalem, the church leaders are no doubt a bit skeptical. And so they send two representatives named John and Peter to investigate. On discovering it is true, the two men remain in Samaria to pray that these new believers receive the infilling of the Holy Spirit. In fact, they lay hands on the Samaritans as they pray. Imagine it—Jews touching Samaritans! And then, *God* touches Samaritans!

But now, who is this John? Could this be the same John of whom we read in Luke 9? Is this the same disciple who hated Samaritans and wanted to destroy them with fire? **Yes, it is!** But how can it be? How is it that before, he wanted to kill them, and now he wants to bless them? How is it possible that he's actually placing his hands on Samaritans and perhaps even pleading in tears for God to baptize them in the Holy Spirit? What happened between Luke 9 and Acts 8 that brought about such a transformation in John's attitude?

The answer is the outpouring of the Holy Spirit on the Day of Pentecost (Acts 2:1-4). John was there when "they were all together in one place" and when "they were all filled with the Holy Spirit and began to speak in other tongues...." When John is filled with the Holy Spirit, he is filled not only with the power of the Spirit, but also with the fruit of the Spirit, the first of which is love. It is God's love poured out by God's Spirit (Romans 5:5) that changed John's life and his attitude. It is this indwelling love that aligned John's heart with the heart of God for the lost.

Peter at the House of Cornelius (Acts 10:1-48)

God was advancing His kingdom. Up to this point the Church was primarily Jewish. The Gentile world needed to be reached, but there were many barriers. Cornelius was a Roman army officer. He was religious and devout. He was a man of prayer and generosity. Cornelius had a vision and saw an angel. The angel offered no criticism or rebuke. Rather, he said, "God has heard your prayer" (NIV). And he advised Cornelius to send for Peter. God is still using angelic visitations, dreams, and visions today, especially among Muslims. When God desires to do a new work, He often has to begin in the heart of the disciple. Peter had a desire to do the work of God, but tradition and prejudice hindered him.

God spoke to Peter three times through a vision, saying, "If God says something is clean, you should not say it is unclean" (author's paraphrase). This was God's way of helping Peter understand that God is no respecter of persons and that God accepts people from every nation that fear Him and do what is right. While Peter contemplated the meaning of the vision, the messengers from Cornelius arrived to invite Peter to Caesarea. When Peter arrived at the home of Cornelius, he found a group of people ready to receive his message.

The effect of the vision in Peter's life is seen when he addressed Cornelius, "I am only a man myself." Peter now understood that being Jewish did not make him superior. In verses 36-44, we have a very interesting New Testament example of Holy Spirit-anointed preaching. It speaks of the good news of peace through Jesus Christ. It clearly speaks of Jesus as Lord of all, the one whom God anointed with the Holy Spirit and who brought healing and deliverance to those under the power of the devil. Peter also clearly proclaims the

Lord's death and resurrection. He proceeds to say that God has appointed Jesus to be the Judge of the living and the dead. All these are important points of the gospel message. Then Peter says, "... everyone who believes in him (Jesus) receives forgiveness of sins" (v. 43). Let us emulate the excellent content of this sermon in our own witness to Muslims.

While Peter was proclaiming the gospel to this assembled group, the Spirit of God was powerfully at work in their hearts and minds. Peter did not give an invitation. He did not even finish preaching the message. God had a different schedule. He interrupted the proceedings: "While Peter was still speaking these words, the Holy Spirit came on all who heard the message" (v. 44, NIV). The Jewish believers were astonished, "for they heard them speaking in tongues and praising God" (v. 46, NIV).

They should not have been astonished because the things that happened were exactly as Jesus had explained to them in Acts 1:8: "You will be my witnesses in Jerusalem and in all Judea and Samaria, and to the end of the earth." From the beginning, the Lord's expressed purpose was to give the good news to *all* people. The Church had taken a great step forward when they began to share the gospel with the Gentile world. It had happened because of the obedience of His followers. Today, the Lord wants to reach Muslims through us. We must begin to understand the practical application of Luke 19:10: "For the Son of Man came to seek and to save the lost."

Think about your answers to the following questions: How does our identity as Americans interface with our identity as disciples of Jesus? Which takes precedence? As good citizens, we understand that some countries are involved in military conflict with militant Muslims. As Christians, we understand that we are supposed to love all people, even our enemies. Can we reconcile this dilemma? We will need to if we are to effectively minister to Muslims.

CONCLUSION

In this lesson our challenge is to love Muslims with the love of God by putting aside wrong attitudes. The biblical examples should not only inform or challenge us, but also encourage us. God's love can be reflected through us to those Muslims we befriend. These words of an individual who works among Muslims challenge us: "Muslims will respond to love. Can we see them as being desperate for the Lord?"

Prayer Points:

- Pray that any negative attitudes toward Muslims would be replaced with true and godly attitudes.

- Pray for a genuine burden for Muslims.

- Pray that God would give each of us a special Muslim friend.

Action Steps:

- Take the initiative when you hear negative reports regarding Muslims by immediately praying for them.

- Search for opportunities to encounter Muslims so you can share Jesus with them.

Review Questions:

1. Based on what you have learned, how will you respond the next time you hear negative reports about Muslims and violence?

2. Thinking about Jonah and his desire for mercy for himself (2:1), but not for Nineveh (4:2-3), discuss this question: "Is it possible for Christians today to have this same double standard toward Muslims?"

3. Read Revelation 5:9 and reflect on God's concern for Muslims to be saved. Why should you be concerned? Do you see Muslims as being lost?

4. What will you do to make it possible for you to have a genuine love for Muslim people?

NOTES

NOTES

GLOBAL INITIATIVE
REACHING **MUSLIM** PEOPLES

NOTES

NOTES

COMPELLED BY LOSTNESS

The objective for Lesson 2 is:

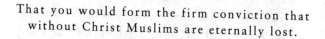

That you would form the firm conviction that
without Christ Muslims are eternally lost.

CHAPTER SUMMARY

In this lesson we will focus on what the Bible teaches about all men needing a Savior and who that Savior is: "there is salvation in no one else, for there is no other name under heaven given among men by which we must be saved" (Acts 4:12). It is only through knowledge about and relationship with Jesus that mankind can find eternal peace. Only when we understand the bad news does the Good News (the gospel) make sense. Simply stated, Jesus died on the cross for our sin. Islam, like other religions, focuses on performing good deeds—with the hope of pleasing Allah enough to escape his judgment. Christianity teaches us that we cannot save ourselves. We need someone who is perfect to pay our penalty before we can stand justified before God. We will examine the differences between the faith and ritual of Muslims and Christians, discussing concepts that will enable us to dialogue with Muslim friends and better understand their perspective on sin and salvation.

CHAPTER OUTLINE

The Muslim Environment

    Testimony

    Dialogue: Are we on the same path?

    Discussion Questions about This Narrative

    We See Their Lostness

What Muslims Must Do: The Pillars of Islam

    The Islamic Creed, the Testimony of Faith

    Prayer

    The Fast

    Almsgiving

    Pilgrimage

    Struggle/Effort (Jihad)

What Muslims Must Believe: The Articles of Faith

    Allah

    Angels

    Books of Allah

    Messengers of Allah

    The Last Day

    Allah's Sovereignty

Why Muslims Are Eternally Lost

    Allah's Attributes Are Misleading

    Man's Sinfulness

    The Cross, "The Stumbling Stone"

Critical Differences Between Islamic and Christian Views

The Two Most Important Questions about Jesus

Who Is Jesus?

Why Did He Come to Earth?

What Islam Teaches about Jesus

Conclusion: Our Obligation to the Lost

Pray and Change

Prayer Points

Action Steps

Review Questions

THE MUSLIM ENVIRONMENT

When Christians think about reaching out to Muslims, they are prone to see only the difficulties and enormity of the task. A common reaction is to think, *They are past the point of no return; conversion for Muslims is impossible.* As a result, we can be defeated before we ever meet our first Muslim friend.

We can deal with this in a couple of ways. First, realize that when a Muslim or any sinner comes to faith in Christ, God has done a great miracle. Second, realize that Satan has blinded them and he does not want to relinquish his influence. See their condition as God sees it—all people without Christ are eternally lost. And Christ's invitation for salvation includes Muslims.

What are the crucial differences in beliefs and practices between Islam and Christianity? How do Muslims view Jesus and the issue of human sin? The answer to these questions will be the major concern of this lesson.

Testimony

Faisal was born and raised in Pakistan. "I was always brought up to oppose the deity of Jesus. The Quran talked about Jesus, but we could never call him the Son of God. That was blasphemy. In fact that was the greatest sin that a Muslim could ever commit—to confess that Jesus was the Son of God. That was the mindset I was brought up with."

After moving to Canada and going into business, he says, "I went to a Christian business conference and they said that Jesus is the Son of God and anyone who calls on His name would have the right to be a child of God." Here, Faisal says, he had a vision of God. "I thought, *Why would God manifest himself among a people who were blaspheming by worshiping Jesus?* Then I heard an audible voice. He said, 'No, these are my children.' When He said that, it was as if a veil fell from my eyes. Then I knew with every fiber of my being that Jesus is the Son of God."

Dialogue: Are we on the same path?

[John]: Hello there. If you don't mind, I'd like to give you this brochure that tells about Jesus Christ. You know, it's really important for people to believe in Jesus in order to go to heaven.

[Salim]: Well thank you so much, but I already believe in Jesus. You see, I'm a Muslim. My name is Salim. Yes, we Muslims believe in Jesus. We believe he is not only a prophet, but a special messenger of Allah. And we too believe that his birth was miraculous, that he was born of a virgin. And we too believe he was a great healer. In fact, our scriptures tell us that he not only healed the blind and the lepers, but raised people from the dead. And we too believe that someday Jesus will return to the world to rule the earth by Allah's Law. So you see, we believe in Jesus and pray to the same god Jesus did.

[John]: Wow! I didn't know all that. I thought Muslims were all pagans, and that you worship the moon-god.

[Salim]: Oh no! We worship the God of Abraham, the great creator of the universe! Yes, we believe in Allah, in angels, in holy books, in prophets, and in the Day of Judgment that will lead to heaven or to hell. And like you, we pray, we fast, and we give to charity. You see, we are like you; we are believers. You do not have to convert us. We already honor Allah and Jesus. We are brothers. And so let's live in peaceful coexistence.

[John]: Wow! I really learned something today. I actually

thought Muslims were all godless fanatics. But now I see that I was totally misled. I can see now that we really are on the same path, and that I don't need to be bothering you. I need to go find the heathen—those who don't know about God and never heard about Jesus. Thank you for setting me straight. Hey, I don't know if I'll ever see you again, but anyway, see ya some day in heaven! So long.

Discussion Questions about This Narrative:

1. Is a brochure (or tract) the best way to start a dialogue with a Muslim?

2. What is the difference in meaning of the key word "believe" for John and Salim?

3. What do you think about Salim's statement, "[We] pray to the same god Jesus did"?

4. Why do you think Salim said to John, "You do not have to convert us"?

5. What do you think about John's final statement to Salim, "See ya some day in heaven"?

6. What key questions has John failed to ask Salim about his supposed faith in Jesus?

We See Their Lostness

Why must we care about Muslims? It's simple: because God cares! The purpose for the coming of Jesus was to bring mankind back into relationship with God.

The story of the first couple, when properly understood by Muslims, is one of the most effective witnessing tools we have to reach Muslims. They need to hear the full story of Creation and the Garden to begin to understand the importance of what Jesus did. They need to learn that in the beginning man had uninterrupted fellowship with God. After man sinned, he hid from God's presence. But God went seeking for mankind. Since that time the pattern has not changed: man, because of his sin, tries to hide from God, but a loving God continues to seek sinners to reestablish His relationship with them. We seek the lost because that is the heart of God. Because of Christ man can once again have fellowship with God.

Look at question three from the above skit. Do we really pray to the same god as Salim says? Since we both believe there is only one "God," it would appear that we are speaking of the same God. However, we have strongly divergent views. In this respect, we speak of a different God. Therefore, we refer to the Muslim god as Allah in this book.

Muslims conceive of Allah as being entirely transcendent (distant from man) and unknowable. He is a god of absolute unity and is predominantly a god of power. Though Muslims place strong emphasis on the merciful and compassionate nature of Allah, they see him as unrestrained and capable of capricious (unpredictable, changeable, impulsive) acts as well.

Christians believe God is primarily a God of love. Thus, His acts are not capricious; that would violate His character. Though He is one God, He exists in three persons. In addition, God is immanent (near to us), first through Jesus the Word of God who descended in the flesh, and second, through the Holy Spirit of God who is now present with those who are redeemed. Therefore, even though we may seem to speak of the same Supreme Being as the orthodox Muslim, when we pray, the God to whom we pray is far different from the god conceptualized by the orthodox Muslim.

Perhaps the question we should be asking is: "How can Muslims come to know God revealed by Jesus, and how can they develop a full understanding of His wonderful love?" Answering that question, and acting on the answer, should be our greatest concern. Let us examine the practices and beliefs of Muslims that contribute to their lostness.

WHAT MUSLIMS MUST DO: THE PILLARS OF ISLAM

A good Muslim must fulfill specific religious obligations, which amount to good works. These religious works are the critical pillars that bind the Islamic community together, providing solidarity, meaning, and preservation. A Muslim's commitment to Islam is measured more by what he does than by what he believes. What he believes is an internal matter, but what he does by way of religious works provides external evidence of his Islamic identity and devotion. Muslims also view religious works as a prerequisite to salvation. According to the Quran, if those good works outweigh their bad works, they will have a greater chance for Paradise. The Pillars of Islam are the following:

The Islamic Creed, the Testimony of Faith

Every Muslim is obligated to recite a prescribed testimony of Islamic faith called the *shahada*. Its words are simple: "I bear witness that there is no god but Allah and I bear witness that Muhammad is the messenger of Allah." When a person utters these words, he identifies himself as a Muslim—one who fully embraces the religion of Islam, the prophet of Islam, and the community of Islam. The words of the *shahada* are often the first words a Muslim hears at birth and the last words he hears at death. The *shahada* is a non-biblical covenant that binds Muslims to the life and example of Muhammad.

Prayer

Though Muslims pray five times a day, they do not view prayer as a time of intimate communion with Allah. Rather, they view prayer as a religious exercise during which they express their devotion and submission to Allah. Allah's majesty and power demand that the prayer be precise and meticulous. As a result, Muslims stress the physical aspects of prayer. These include time, location, preparation, direction, wording, and posture. Muslims must perform their prayers at specifically designated times of the day marked by a prayer call that is chanted through the loudspeaker of a local mosque. Muslims can choose to pray in their homes, but their traditions promise greater merit for prayer in the mosque. Upon entering the prayer hall, Muslims must remove their shoes and perform a ceremonial washing. When they are ready to pray, they must face in the direction of Mecca and recite their prayers in Arabic. Their prayers consist mainly of verses from the Quran and words which Muhammad supposedly prayed over thirteen centuries ago. Prayer postures include standing, bowing, kneeling, and prostration. **We see the attention, the detail, and the reverence Muslims give to prayer.**

The Fast

Muslims are required to keep a special fast during the ninth month of the Muslim calendar known as Ramadan. According to Islamic teaching, the month of Ramadan is a holy month because it is the month when they believe the angel Gabriel began to deliver the revelation of the Quran to Muhammad. Muslims begin the month-long fast when they see the new moon that marks the beginning of the month. They fast from dawn until sunset of each day, abstaining from food, liquid, sex, and even smoking. For most Muslims throughout the world, fasting during Ramadan is an extremely rigorous exercise. However, it is an exercise that bonds the worldwide community of Islam as Muslims bear this hardship together.

Almsgiving

Every Muslim is obligated to contribute toward the social and religious needs of the community by means of almsgiving. Muslims call this requirement *zakat*. Islamic teaching is clear about helping the poor, the orphan, and the widow. It requires Muslims to give 2.5% of their earnings to charity, which in many cases is collected by the government. The government then distributes the funds for humanitarian causes, such as orphanages, hospitals and feeding programs. It also distributes the funds for religious causes, such as the building and maintenance of mosques and religious schools.

Pilgrimage

Every Muslim is obligated to perform a special pilgrimage to Mecca, Saudi Arabia. This should occur at least once in his lifetime if he is financially able. The pilgrimage rituals take place during the twelfth month, *Dhu'l Hijja*, and last for several days. The pilgrimage (known as the *hajj*) provides the Muslim with the opportunity to visit the most sacred of Islam's holy sites, Al-Masjid Al-Haram (The Sacred Mosque) in Mecca, Saudi Arabia. This is a mosque complex that encloses the cube-shaped shrine known as the Kaaba, which Muslims view as the "House of Allah." There the pilgrims congregate to praise Allah. According to Islamic tradition, Abraham and Ishmael laid the foundation of the Kaaba after which time Allah instituted the pilgrimage as a lasting ordinance. Nowadays, as many as two million Muslims converge on Mecca each year to perform the pilgrimage.

Struggle/Effort (Jihad)

Some Muslims add *jihad* to this list of religious obligations. For Muslims, it refers to a variety of personal experiences that involve effort or struggle. For example, some Muslims speak in terms of a jihad of the soul, jihad of the hand, jihad of the tongue, or jihad of the sword. "Jihad of the soul" bears the most important meaning; it refers to the spiritual struggle of overcoming the temptations of Satan. "Jihad of the hand" refers to perseverance against the physical hardships of life. "Jihad of the tongue" refers to the perseverance of sharing one's Islamic faith through dialogue or debate. "Jihad of the sword" refers to the Muslim's obligation to defend Islam even if it means by the sword of combat.

A missionary listened as his Muslim professor gave his reason for not praying and not keeping the Islamic fast. The missionary asked, "Aren't you a Muslim?" He responded firmly, "I am a [his national citizenship], therefore I am a Muslim!" Just because a Muslim doesn't practice their faith does not change their religious identity nor the fact that they are lost.

WHAT MUSLIMS MUST BELIEVE: THE ARTICLES OF FAITH

For Muslims, faith is primarily an intellectual process of acknowledging as true the teachings of the Quran and its prophet. This knowledge in itself becomes a fulfillment of one of the requirements of salvation. Thus, to be a good Muslim, one must believe in the following articles of faith:

Allah

Muslims must believe there is only one god who is referred to as Allah. This is the fundamental tenet of Islam—the absolute oneness of Allah. This god is the lord of heaven and earth and shares his power and deity with no other. He exists from eternal past to eternal future. He was never begotten, nor does he beget another. And he is the creator of all things including humans whom he fashioned to worship him.

Angels

Muslims must believe in angels who are spirit beings created by Allah from pure light. While humans live in the earthly realm, angels live in the heavenly realm where they serve and worship in the presence of Allah. They provide an indirect link between Allah and humans in that they bring Allah's blessings down from heaven, they intercede on behalf of humans, and they deliver Allah's messages. The most prominent angel is known by the Arabic name *Jibril*, Gabriel in the Christian faith.

Books of Allah

Muslims must believe that, over time, Allah provided guidance to humankind in the form of divine revelations which were revealed and recorded in scripture for the benefit of the human race. According to Muslims, there were four major revelations or holy books that descended from heaven. In chronological order, they were the *Tawrat, Zabur, Injil,* and Quran. The first three correspond to the Torah, the Psalms, and the Gospel (New Testament). The last revelation, the Quran, instructs Muslims to believe in all the previous revelations.

Say you: "*We believe in Allah, and the revelation given to us, and to Abraham, Isma'il, Jacob, and the Tribes, and that given to Moses and Jesus, and that given to (all) Prophets from their Lord. We make no difference between one and another of them*" *(Quran 2:136).*

However, Muslims regard the Quran as the best revelation because it was the last and most up-to-date version of Allah's will for the world. For Muslims, the Quran displaces all previous books of scripture and renders them outdated, unnecessary, and even annulled.

Messengers of Allah

Muslims must believe that Allah chose certain people to serve as prophets to receive and convey his message to humankind. The four prophets who received one of the four major holy books bear the title "Messenger of Allah." According to Muslims, a prophet named Moses received the Tawrat; another named David received the Zabur; one named Jesus, the Injil; and the fourth named Muhammad, the Quran. Of course, we recognize the first three names as major biblical figures. The Quran mentions many other prophets by their Arabic names. As the following list demonstrates, most of these names resemble biblical names.

Adam	Ismail (Ishmael)	Sulaiman (Solomon)
Idris (Enoch)	Yaqub (Jacob)	Yunus (Jonah)
Nuh (Noah)	Yusuf (Joseph)	Ilyas (Elijah)
Ayub (Job)	Shu'aib (Jethro)	Al-Yasa (Elisha)
Ibrahim (Abraham)	Harun (Aaron)	Zakaria (Zechariah)
Ishaq (Isaac)	Talut (Saul)	Yahya (John the Baptist)

Because the Quranic narratives appear similar to the biblical accounts, some Christians believe that some of the material in the Quran was borrowed from Jewish and Christian sources. It's important to know that Muslims believe that, because Muhammad is chronologically the last in the list of prophets and messengers, he is esteemed as the greatest; he received the latest of Allah's guidance. Therefore he is the one to be followed, not any other.

The Last Day

Muslims must believe in the Last Day—a resurrection and judgment that will mark the end of the world. The Quran teaches that Allah will raise the dead to life and judge them on the basis of their deeds and his mercy. While the details of this event are not clear, what is clear is that some people will be admitted into a place called Paradise, and others will be cast into a place called Hell. Muslims believe Paradise is a place of eternal reward. It is a garden of bliss in heaven where pure rivers flow. It is a place where beautiful heavenly companions will serve men and women to their heart's delight. The residents of Paradise will be able to enjoy in greater abundance all the good and physical pleasures Allah intended for them on earth, as well as other activities that are forbidden on earth, such as drinking alcohol. They will be dressed in silk robes, recline on soft cushions, and feast on bountiful fruit. Hell, on the other hand, is a place of terrible punishment—a place of fire and torment. The guilty will be bound in chains and suffer the agony of boiling water on their heads and hooked irons in their flesh.

Allah's Sovereignty

Muslims must believe Allah is sovereign over all things, including good and evil. Nothing controls Allah; rather, everything is under his control. For Muslims, this means that Allah determines in advance (predestines) both the acts and condition of every human being. Each one's fate is written; it is fixed and none can change it. This belief leads to a fatalistic mindset which offers no hope for change. Although people appear completely helpless as far as their lives are concerned, Muslims believe that Allah will still hold them accountable for their actions on Judgment Day.

As we shall see in lesson three, most Muslims are not content to yield to this fatalistic approach to life. When confronted with a crisis, they are not satisfied with the response of formal Islam: "It is Allah's will." And because formal Islam offers no hope for change, many Muslims embrace a different expression of Islam known as Folk Islam, which opens the door to occult practices and powers.

WHY MUSLIMS ARE ETERNALLY LOST

The Muslim view of Allah will help us understand why they reject the biblical remedy for sin—the blood of the Cross and the resurrection of Jesus.

Allah's Attributes Are Misleading

When Muslims think of Allah, they think of him as primarily a god of power. That is why the rallying cry of Islam heard round the world is *"Allahu Akbar, Allahu Akbar"*—Allah is greater, Allah is greater! No matter what kind of power one can imagine—hydropower, solar power, nuclear power—Allah is more powerful. Allah is greater. Among all the traits attributed to Allah, Muslims view power as his most dominant one. Unfortunately, this premise leads to several significant misleading conclusions.

Allah is inaccessible. For the Muslim, the greater his authority, the greater his majesty. The greater his majesty, the greater the distance between him and all others. Imagine the status of a CEO working in an office building. If the building has twenty floors, most likely the CEO would have his office on the twentieth floor, far removed from the ordinary citizen on the street. The ordinary citizen would rarely get to meet with the CEO. In the same way, Allah's majesty demands that he be far removed from ordinary man. Allah is accessible only to the prophets and Muslim saints.

Allah is also impersonal. Because he is all-powerful, he is master over everything. The Quran states that no one can come to Allah except as a servant. The only relationship humans can have with Allah is that of servant to master. There can never be any intimacy, only a relationship of servitude. That's why Muslims are offended when Christians speak in terms of becoming the children of God. For Muslims, that implies a horizontal relationship that drags Allah down to the level of humanity—something Muslims view as insulting to the exalted glory of Allah.

Allah is unpredictable. Nothing can restrain or constrain him, not even a code of ethics distinguishing right from wrong. If Allah were limited by some moral law, then that law would have control over him. But that can never be for the Muslim. Allah is not even bound by promises. Otherwise, in similar fashion, the promise would have control over Allah. **This is why a Muslim can never be certain of salvation.** Allah can change his mind for any reason and is accountable to no one. No wonder Muslims worship Allah in fear. They can never know which direction he will turn. He is like the wind—unpredictable! As it says in the Quran, "Allah forgives whom he pleases, and punishes whom he pleases" (Quran 5:18).

Man's Sinfulness

The most significant misleading concept is that Allah is immune to human sin. Muslims believe in sin and hell, but in a way different from the Christian view. Because humans are created with the capacity to worship Allah, Muslims insist that everyone is born good. For Muslims, sin is not a *condition* but a *commission*. In other words, humans are not born in a state of sin; rather, because of human imperfections and corrupted environment, they *commit* acts of sin and *become* sinners. It's the environment that needs to be transformed. Because people are born good, there is no need for any spiritual transformation. What is needed, claims the Muslim, is guidance from Allah to help humans know how to fix the environment.

When Muslims commit sins, they do not experience a sense of personal transgression against God. There is nothing similar to the anguish of Psalm 51:1–4: "O God ... against you, you only, have I sinned...." Because Allah is far removed, he is not adversely affected by the Muslim's shortcomings, and neither is the Muslim's relationship with Allah. Allah remains the Master, far aloof in his royal realm of power and majesty, and the Muslim remains his servant. This wide gap of separation is not seen as a result of sin; it is simply because of who Allah is and who man is. That is why a Christian's explanation about sin separating man from God is difficult for a Muslim to grasp.

In Islam, Allah is not only powerful; he is just. Thus, he has set in place a system of justice whereby any wrong can be rectified by payment of a penalty. According to Muslim belief, Allah in his mercy provides a means by which Muslims can fulfill the requirement of justice and atone for their sins. This provision consists basically of good works—saying extra prayers, fasting extra days, feeding the poor, giving to charity, and practicing the Pillars of Islam.

The Quran declares, "For those things that are good remove those things that are evil" (11:114). By now it should be clear why the religion of Islam is so works oriented, and why knowledge of the Law (what is permissible and what is not) is so critical. The Muslim's salvation depends on it. Muslims believe they have the capability to atone for their own personal sin. Thus, they see no need for the Christian Cross. They not only dismiss any need for the Cross, they adamantly reject it!

The Cross, "The Stumbling Stone"

From a Muslim's point of view, the Christian's viewpoint is unthinkable. It is abject ignorance to believe in a story which speaks of Jesus (Islam's second-greatest prophet) as abandoned by God and left in the hands of pagan soldiers to be humiliated on a cross. For Muslims, the Cross represents a weak Christian God, not powerful enough to rescue one of His own. For a Muslim whose Allah is all-powerful, such a story is ridiculous. In fact, it is demeaning to the exalted majesty of Allah; it is blasphemous.

This rejection on the part of Muslims brings us to the great divide. Our greatest separation is about the most critical issue of all—the remedy for sin. The Muslim contends for forgiveness through the merit of human works. The Christian seeks atonement through the blood of the Cross. One adamantly rejects the Cross. The other gives his life for it.

It is the biblical view of God that brings us to this impasse. Though Christians acknowledge God's omnipotence, the gospel reveals a far more profound truth—God's predominant attribute is not power; it is love. This is what accounts for the vast difference between the Muslim and Christian worldviews. For example, because God is love (1 John 4:8), Christians do not see Him residing in some aloof corner of the universe, far removed from the human race. Instead, He is searching in the "garden," calling out to Adam, "Where are you?" Because God is love, He wants to have an intimate relationship with humanity, whereby we become His children, and He our Heavenly Father. Because His love dominates, all that He does is constrained by love. In this way, He is predictable. We can be sure His power will serve only for the good of creation, and whatever He does will be born of His mercy and compassion. His power will always be subject to His love. And because God is love, because He is near, and because He deeply cares, our sins do affect Him. This is clearly revealed in the story of Noah. God was deeply concerned about the affairs of the world, and as He looked upon humankind, He saw the depravity of sin. Notice now how the Scriptures vividly describe God's reaction: "The LORD saw that the wickedness of man was great in the earth, and that every intention of the thoughts of his heart was only evil continually. And the LORD regretted that he had made man on the earth, and it grieved him to his heart" (Gen. 6:5-6).

For the Muslim, the idea that Allah could suffer such pain of heart is both absurd and revolting. But Christian Scriptures differ, revealing the wonderful truth that God is first a God of love. Any loving parent can identify to some degree with this grief, especially when a child rebels. Because God is lovingly near, our sins are not committed only against one another; they are committed against Him. We dishonor His righteousness. We violate His holiness. We pierce the heart of a loving God who yearns for our fellowship. Is there anything we mortal beings can do to heal the broken heart of God? Of course not. There is no way we could atone for such a grievous crime. All we can do is rely on God's mercy. And God who is merciful devised a way for this penalty to be paid, a penalty that we could never afford. Christ's suffering on the Cross fulfilled the requirement of divine justice. This is God's gift to the world—Jesus the Savior, in whose blood there is atonement, forgiveness, and remission of sin.

This brings us to two crucial observations. First, we must realize that God has provided only one path of salvation, and that path leads through the blood Jesus shed on the Cross. To deny or circumvent the sacrificial death of Jesus is to deny God's gift of salvation. Without this sole provision of salvation, people remain lost and eternally doomed. It is not enough to believe in a creator-god. It is not enough to believe that Jesus was a great prophet. Muslims must embrace Jesus as Savior of the world and Lord of their lives. Otherwise, they too are eternally lost. Muslims must call on the name of the Lord to be saved. But "how then will they call on him in whom they have not believed? And how are they to believe in him of whom they have never heard? And how are they to hear without someone preaching?" (Romans 10:14). That's where Christians come in. God has granted us the privilege of proclaiming the Good News that there is a Savior in whose name there is forgiveness of sins!

The second crucial observation is this: In most cases, the only way Muslims will come to accept the message of the Cross is by perceiving God as a God of love. Unless they see this face of God, the Cross will remain a stumbling block. It is this face that Jesus came to reveal, the face of the Father, Yahweh, who is described in Exodus 33 by the twin attributes of mercy and compassion. But Jesus is no longer physically here on earth revealing this face of His Father. Where will Muslims find, see or observe this divine love? Where will they see this mercy and compassion revealed? Hopefully, they'll find it flowing out of the hearts of those in whom Jesus continues to dwell.

CRITICAL DIFFERENCES BETWEEN ISLAMIC AND CHRISTIAN VIEWS

Term	Muslim View	Christian View
1. God	(*Allah*) All-powerful, distant, impersonal, unpredictable, immune to human behavior	All-loving, accessible, personal, covenantal, moved by human behavior
2. Christ	Prophet only to Children of Israel	Son of God, Savior of the World
3. Trinity	Christians have three separate gods (God, Mary, and Jesus)	Father, Son, and Holy Spirit (Three-in-one)
4. Scripture	Quran, revelation from Allah, supersedes biblical Scripture	Bible, revelation from God, authoritative and final
5. Sin	Human weakness corrupted by the environment; shame	Inherent condition brought on by Adam's fall; guilt

Term	Muslim View	Christian View
6. Salvation	Requirement: faith and human works; no assurance	Requirement: faith and the work of Christ; absolute assurance
7. Faith	Object: Allah and Muhammad	Object: The Lord Jesus Christ
8. Piety	Emphasis on obedience to ritual	Emphasis on sanctification by the Holy Spirit
9. Supernatural powers	Allah, angels, Satan, earthly spirits (*jinn*), both good and bad	God, angels, demons (fallen angels)
10. Heaven	Eternal fulfillment of all earthly pleasures intended by Allah	Eternal fellowship with God in the spiritual realm

THE TWO MOST IMPORTANT QUESTIONS ABOUT JESUS

There are two eternally important questions about Jesus that Muslims **do not** correctly answer. Jesus first confronted His disciples with the first questions in Matthew 16:13-16. That question was "Who do people say that the Son of Man is?" The second question is "Why did Jesus come to earth?"

Who Is Jesus?

Jesus asked what the people were saying about His identity. Their opinions included John the Baptist, Elijah,

Jeremiah, or one of the other prophets. "He said to them, 'But who do you say that I am?'"

In the original Greek, the word "you" is emphasized by being placed at the beginning of the sentence. Peter, as spokesman for the group, answers Jesus with these words: "You are the Christ (Messiah), the Son of the living God." The words "Messiah" and "Christ" have the same meaning: "anointed by God" or "God's chosen one." This is based on the Jewish practice of anointing a new ruler with oil to show he was God's choice to be king over Israel.

Why Did He Come to Earth?

Matthew states early in the Gospel narrative (Matthew 1:21): "She will bear a son, and you shall call his name Jesus, for he will save his people from their sins." Jesus also taught that He came to die for sin, not to immediately establish an earthly kingdom. Matthew records this statement after Peter's confession of faith (Matthew 16:21). He lays out God's plan: He will suffer and die at the hands of the religious leaders, then conquer death by rising from the dead! His purpose becomes clear at the Crucifixion. As Jesus hangs between the two thieves on the Cross (Luke 23:39-43, NKJV), one asks to be delivered from death. He says, "If You are the Christ, save Yourself and us." The other thief recognizes who Jesus is—the innocent and sinless Messiah.

Jesus was (and is) the Son of God—God's exact choice to be a perfect sacrifice, Priest, King, and Savior of the world. The second thief asks to be remembered when Jesus rules in His future kingdom. *He expresses faith in who Jesus is.* Jesus responds with the great promise "today you will be with Me in Paradise." This thief knew he could not save himself; he could do no righteous acts to persuade God to forgive him; he would be dead in a few hours. Jesus promises him forgiveness on the basis of God's grace, and His work on the Cross, neither of which the thief deserved.

So we have these two important questions and their answers: 1. "Who is Jesus?" The Bible says He is the Son of God. 2. "Why did He come to earth?" He came to die as the atoning sacrifice for the sin of all mankind, if they will only believe. The answers a person gives to these questions will determine where he or she will spend eternity. This is not just head knowledge but truth that must be experienced. The questions must be answered in only one order. One must first see who Jesus is and only then does His death have any purpose. Next we will consider the objections Muslims bring to these answers.

WHAT ISLAM TEACHES ABOUT JESUS

What then does Islam say concerning these two critical questions? Concerning the person of Jesus, they say He is merely a prophet of Allah, who was surpassed in importance by Muhammad. They believe that Muhammad is the final prophet in time and importance; his words supersede those of all previous prophets. This was necessary, they believe, because the true message of Allah was corrupted by Christians.

In the previous narrative, Salim noted five things about Jesus that Muslims hold to be true and amazing: the birth of Jesus was miraculous; he was born of a virgin and born sinless; he was a great healer; he ascended to Allah, without dying; and, someday Jesus will return to rule the earth by Allah's Law.

Though Muhammad did not get all the facts straight, these very concepts point to the uniqueness of our Lord. This can be the basis for questions leading to a fuller understanding of His identity. The fact that Jesus is virgin born and sinless could suggest questions such as:

1. "If Jesus has no earthly father, who was His father?"

2. "Why do Scriptures note the sinless nature of Jesus?"

3. "If Jesus is the only prophet with the gift of healing from God and Jesus did not die (their belief), is He still able to heal people today?"

4. "When Jesus comes to earth again, will He be subject to death here?"

5. "Will Jesus also be involved in the judgment of mankind?"

The above questions might encourage Muslims to think beyond what they usually do when the subject of Jesus is discussed.

CONCLUSION:
OUR OBLIGATION TO THE LOST

We have seen that we have an obligation to tell Muslims who Jesus is and what He did when He came to earth. Is there more to our obligation than this? Yes. We need also to demonstrate God's character. Besides knowing God's truth, Muslims need to encounter God's love and power. This is needed because the truth can appear cold and impersonal to Muslims, especially when it contradicts what they have always believed. How can we fulfill the obligation to love Muslims? How can we change some of our behavior and attitudes toward followers of Islam?

Pray and Change

If our knowledge of Muslims is based mainly on the mass media, we are likely to have a distorted and negative view of them. If we do not have any friends outside of our cultural group we may be in danger of being ethnocentric. This can make it hard to imagine ourselves speaking with Muslims who are outside our comfort zone. It is easy to affirm that what they do, teach, and believe is all wrong. They come from strange and different lands, have their own music, eat unique food, and generally have a different lifestyle. The truth is, they are not strange; they are just different.

Before we can share the love of Christ with them, we must make an effort to understand such differences. Then we need to change, ask God to forgive us for being culturally self-centered, and develop an attitude of love for Muslims. God has promised to help us change. Carl Ellis said: "We should always remember that Islam is a system, but Muslims are people. We may not like the system, but people we must love."[2] Muslims will respond to love!

Prayer Points:

- Pray that we will develop relationships with Muslims.

- Pray that Muslims will understand how sin (not fate) distances them from pleasing God.

- Pray that Muslims will be dissatisfied with the rituals of Islam.

Action Steps:

- Ask your Muslim friend how or what they do when they pray.

- Find and read some testimonies of Muslims who have come to saving faith in Christ and note their responses to the Cross. One good source is www.answering-islam.org.

Review Questions:

1. Why are Muslims lost?

2. What are four of the major differences between Islam and Christianity?

NOTES

NOTES

NOTES

NOTES

HOLY SPIRIT EMPOWERMENT FOR PROCLAIMING THE GOSPEL

The objective for Lesson 3 is:

That you would be empowered by the Holy Spirit to discern the spiritual forces at work in Islam and to advance the gospel with boldness.

CHAPTER SUMMARY

As we look at the Muslim world from a human perspective, the task of understanding culture, theology, and worldview seems overwhelming. It is. But we are not alone in this endeavor. We have the Holy Spirit to direct and aid us as we seek to bring glory to God. In this lesson, we look at major approaches that we can use as we proclaim the "Good News" to Muslims today. Often the most neglected method is a testimony. Yet it is often the most powerful. It can be your personal testimony or a story of other Muslims or friends who have come to faith. When Jesus was sharing His message, He resorted to three main approaches—storytelling, questions, and power encounters. Breaking through spiritual darkness is key. It is in this darkness that we find lost Muslims who need us to do battle with Satan and the spirit world. In this chapter we learn how Muslims perceive that spirit world and how God is granting victories by opening the door to their hearts. We begin by looking at the kind of encounter Muslims must have—an encounter with the power of God!

CHAPTER OUTLINE

A Working Environment: Biblical Approaches to Muslims

> Testimonies
>
> Stories and Parables
>
> Chronological Bible Storying

Questions

> Responding to Muslim Objections with Questions
>
> Exploration in the Place of Explanation

Changing the Environment

> Folk Islam
>
> Need of a Mediator
>
> Need for Power

"Power Encounters" among Muslims

A Biblical Perspective

How Does Power Encounter Work?

Dreams and Visions

> Biblical Background
>
> Examples from Our Day

The Power of Pentecost

Conclusion

> Prayer Points
>
> Action Steps
>
> Review Questions

A WORKING ENVIRONMENT: BIBLICAL APPROACHES TO MUSLIMS

Testimonies

The story of how Jesus changed your life is your personal testimony. It tells Muslims that you were not born an "authentic" Christian, but that you made a conscious decision to follow Jesus. The Gospels give us many illustrations of people who encountered Jesus and how their story changed the lives of others. Such are the stories of the Gospel of John chapter 1, where many of the future apostles first met Jesus. Also in this Gospel we have the testimony of Nicodemus (John 3).

- ### The Disciples (John 1)

John 1:1-14 relates a testimony from John the apostle where he proclaims Jesus as the Son of the Father. Next, in verses 15-18, is a summary of the testimony from John the Baptist. Starting in verse 19 through verse 34 are the exact words of John the Baptist when the religious leaders in Jerusalem asked his identity. He states he is not the Messiah. In verses 29 and 36, he proclaims that Jesus is the One, the Lamb of God, sent to take away the sins of the world. Having met Jesus himself, Andrew went to get Peter his brother to introduce him to Jesus. His testimony is again about who Jesus is! Later, Philip found Nathanael and did the same. Jesus indicates the power of God allowed Him to see Nathanael under the fig tree before Philip came with the Good News about Jesus. With such information, Nathanael realizes and confesses who Jesus is, the "Son of God ... the King of Israel" (v. 49). Such is the power of personal testimony!

- ### Nicodemus (John 3)

In John 3, verses 1-21, Jesus encounters Nicodemus. He

came because something attracted him to Jesus. "Rabbi, we know that you are a teacher come from God, for no one can do these signs that you do unless God is with him" (v. 2).

Here is a man who was attracted by the signs and wonders that followed the ministry of Jesus. Perhaps Nicodemus had heard about Jesus for quite a while. Now that He was in town, this would be his opportunity to meet Him. He would have to do it after dark, for if he was seen with Jesus, he might be accused of being His disciple. What "miraculous signs" had he seen Jesus do? Perhaps he was there on the day recorded in Luke 5:17-26, when the paralytic was healed. Perhaps Nicodemus heard Jesus tell the man that his sins were forgiven and then watched him walk away carrying his mat. He could have been present in the synagogue the day that the man with the withered hand was healed (Luke 6:6-11). Here Jesus did not even touch the man. The inevitable question formed in his mind, *Who is this man? Perhaps this is the Messiah promised long ago.*

What were the spiritual and mental characteristics of this man Nicodemus? He was a man with an open mind, intellectually honest, and also humble of heart. He had a longing in his heart that had not been satisfied by either his religious activities or positions of leadership. It was this seeking heart that Jesus saw. He went straight to the point. Jesus told him, "Nicodemus, you have seen some of the miracles, but the greatest one, I am going to tell you about now. Nicodemus, you must be 'born again'" (author's paraphrase; John 3:7). Jesus knew that when a message is given in an unexpected way it will have a high impact on the hearers. When people are highly impacted by a message, they are more likely to respond and act upon it.

How does this apply? Some people, especially Muslim people, can be attracted to our message by the supernatural. The event may be a healing, or, especially for Muslims, it may be a dream or vision. It might be a deliverance from demon power and oppression. Jesus did not keep himself or His message secret or hidden. He worked and lived among the people; He ministered to people, praying for their needs. To find receptive people we must be teaching, praying for healings, and seeing deliverance for those bound by Satan. We must be in the midst of the people where these are **visible for all to see.**

Stories and Parables

Jesus used stories and parables all the time. There remains a consistent challenge to tell parables to get truth into the hearts and minds of Muslims. Below are six reasons for stories in outreach situations.

1. Storytelling is a universal form of communication.

    No matter where you travel in this world, people love to tell or hear stories. Whether to emphasize a point, or inject humor, you will probably use a story. Stories can be heard anywhere: in church, the courtroom, the movie theater and even prison. Not only do all people tell stories, they need to hear **your story.**

2. More than half of the world's people prefer to learn orally (by hearing).

    Today the semi-literate and illiterate outnumber the literate people in the world. People in this situation tend to express themselves using oral forms (stories and symbols) instead of with abstract concepts (propositional thinking and philosophy).

3. Stories connect with our imagination and emotions.

    Effective communication touches not only the mind but the heart and emotions as well. One of the best ways to do this is through a story. Think of all the things a story can provide: cheers, tears, anger, sarcasm and hope. Stories draw people into the lives of the characters because stories mirror our own lives and feelings.

4. Every major religion uses stories to socialize their youth, convert unbelievers, and indoctrinate members.

It does not matter which religion you think about, they all use stories to expand or limit membership. All religions use stories to separate the true followers from non-members. Shared stories create community and provide for a non-threatening way to challenge basic beliefs and behavior.

5. Approximately 75 percent of the Bible is narrative.

There are three literary styles that make up the sacred text, approximately: narrative 75%, poetry 15%, and thought-organized 10%. The genre that predominates is narrative with the stories of those who served God and those who served themselves. The Bible was not given to reveal the lives of particular people but rather to reveal the working of God in their lives. Poetry in the Psalms, Proverbs and some prophets provides a way to express deep inner emotions. Stories create instant evangelists.

People find it very easy to repeat a good story. Whether it is gossip, or the gospel of Jesus, something within us wants to repeat a good story. Good stories get retold. When people hear good stories they often retell them immediately to family and friends.

6. Jesus taught theology through stories.

Jesus never wrote a book on systematic theology, yet He taught theology wherever He went. As a holistic thinker, Jesus used parables to tease His audience into reflecting

on new ways of thinking about life. Through His stories,
Jesus challenged His listeners to think, extend mercy
to others, share wealth with the poor, and search for
hidden riches.

Why did Jesus speak so often in parables? The obvious
reason was to communicate effectively. Jesus wanted
people to hear not just with their ears, but also with their
understanding.

The parables of Luke 15 are great illustrations of stories
Jesus told. There are three parables about "lost things."
These three things are: a lost sheep (vv. 3-7), a lost coin
(vv. 8-10), and a lost son (vv. 11-32). In fact, there were
two lost sons in that household, but only one left the home
physically. The purpose of God as described in these parables
tells us that the Father does not want sinners to be lost, but
to be in a living relationship with Him. They also illustrate
the purpose for Jesus coming to this world—to save lost
sinners. The final parable of the three, the Prodigal Son, is a
beautiful illustration to your Muslim friend of how the Father
welcomes all who repent.

Chronological Bible Storying

- *Why teach orally?*

Today, over one-half of all people receive their information
predominantly from oral, non-written sources. That's more
than four billion people. We can call such people oral
communicators because they prefer to learn by hearing instead
of reading. **Many oral learners can read, but are not able to
comprehend or use information from a written source.** They
need to hear in an appropriate format, such as a story, poem
or song, to fully understand and use the information. Being an
oral communicator has nothing to do with intelligence level,
for many of them can read and often speak more than one

language. Orality is simply their preferred method of learning.

The majority of Muslim women are oral communicators. Most Muslim girls are educated using rote memorization and a few years after leaving school, most become functionally illiterate. By contrast, most American women are highly literate, and literate people don't trust the memories of oral communicators. We often look for people who can read the Bible and then we can discuss it with them.

QUESTIONS

Responding to Muslim Objections with Questions

Just as Jesus was confronted with questions, so many Muslims seem to enjoy asking questions of unsuspecting Christians. Many of their questions can be verbal traps. Often these questions are a set-up for them to ridicule some Christian truth and present an argument that many Christians have never heard before. Jesus, when confronted by such questions, responded not with the expected answer, but with **another question**. You can do the same today with Muslims. Here is a list of some of the most commonly asked questions with suggested questions you can ask in response.

- *Definition Questions (Comprehension Questions)*

Consider a modern definition question that a believer might encounter when speaking to a Muslim. The Muslim asks the question "Are you a Christian?" How do you answer such a question? Should there be any hesitation to answer, and if so for what reason? How do you answer this in a non-threatening way?

Following the example of Jesus, you could answer with another question. You could ask, "What do you mean by the word 'Christian'?" Let them define this key word for you, based on their worldview, experience, and the testimony they have received from others.

If you follow this line, you can be sure that they will give only a partially correct answer at best. They may define a Christian as someone who they believe worships three gods, a person who indulges in immorality and loose living as he has seen on American videos, or someone who believes that God had physical relations with Mary in order to produce a son. Your response, to whatever is said, will be important. If the main content of their answer is about what Christians "**do**" in a negative sense, you can state that God has either delivered us from that kind of lifestyle, or He has kept us from such a life by His power. If the content of the answer has to do with what Christians "**believe**," especially about the "Son" of God, again ask, "What is your definition of the word 'Son' in this context?"

Remember, "definition questions" are used with Muslims to determine the meaning of key words which they use in their theological discussions. Many of the common religious terms which Christians use have a different definition in the Muslim context.

• Contrast Questions (Evaluation Questions)

Several years ago, in the West Bank, we were holding a daylong conference for our Muslim correspondence students. They were studying an evangelistic course that was specifically prepared for orthodox Muslim students. We knew we had three types of young men present: some were newly committed to Christ, some were still undecided, and some were Muslim friends who had not studied with us at all, but had come for the free meal and lively discussion. During a time of questions and answers, a Muslim friend decided he would solve this problem of Christianity for everyone with a simple question of the "comprehension" type. He stood and asked, "Which would you rather have to cross the desert with, a brand new four-wheel-drive Jeep, or an old beat up wreck?" The answer seemed obvious, because to cross the desert you want something reliable and new. However, the real question being asked was this: "Which would you rather have, the new religion Islam, or the old religion Christianity?" And everyone in the room understood that this was the question of the day. The real question was an "evaluation" question concerning the two faiths.

A believer in Jesus stood up and posed another question that sounds almost the same, but really was quite different and enabled the people in the room to see the whole issue in a new light. This second question was, "Which would you rather have to *lead* you across the desert, an old guide with years of experience or a young guide?" The image and the real question had now been changed and the answer was completely different. *Now* you want an old guide (the old religion), Christianity. In the desert it is an unquenched thirst that kills, and out there you want someone who knows all the places water can be found. It is the same with religion; you need one that provides real guidance, not one that just claims to be the newest.

Another way to use questions is in comparisons and contrasts. In Luke 5:23, Jesus uses this type of question just before He heals the man who was paralyzed. He asks the crowd of religious people, "Which is easier, to say, 'Your sins are forgiven you,' or to say, 'Rise and walk'?" In this case it was easier to say, "Your sins are forgiven," because there would be no visible change in the man. Jesus therefore does the more difficult, the healing, to prove that He has authority on earth to do both—**to forgive and to heal.**

Such questions start out with a phrase such as ... "Which is easier...," "Which is better...."

Theological questions will arise. Although there are many of these, three main questions that are encountered are:

1. Is Jesus the Son of God?

Again, a "yes" answer will cause a Muslim to believe something about you that is not correct. How do you answer? As before, you can ask for a definition of the key word. "What does the word 'son' mean to you? What are Christians saying when they call Jesus 'Son of God' in your thinking?" He will probably say that Christians believe God had a wife named Mary, with whom he had sexual relations, and Jesus was the result. This is what he has been told Christians believe about Mary, the mother of the "Son of God." You can rightfully be shocked and claim that such a statement is blasphemy! Christians do not believe that Jesus was a biological son of God, but when Muslims hear the word "son" in this context, they respond as they have been trained.

What Christians do believe is that Jesus is the Son in His **relationship** with the Father (John 3:16). The relationship between Jesus and God can best be described by the earthly words "Father" and "Son." You should know that Muslims also use the term "son" to describe relationships in many of their own languages. In Malaysia, the key for opening doors is called the "son of the lock." No birth is intended here, it is just a way to describe a "working relationship" between lock and key. In Egypt, a native is often called a "son of the Nile." This means people from Egypt have their source of life in the Nile River which brings them water, not that the river actually gave birth. There are other examples but the point is that the term "son" is used by Christians in a figurative manner, not in a literal one.

2. Did Christ die on the Cross?

For the Muslim it is a scandalous idea that the great prophet Jesus died on the Cross. To them this is a defeat. It shows a God (to use the Christian term) that is weaker than Satan. Muslims worship power and they cannot conceive of this as being a demonstration of power on the part of God. This is more difficult because Muslims do not understand the reason His death was necessary. Possible questions could be:

"If your death could save your son's life, would you be willing to give your life for his?"

"Do you know that some of the other great prophets suffered because of their work, such as Jeremiah and Isaiah?"

"Do you know the purpose for which Jesus himself said He came to the people of Israel?" (Mark 10:45; Luke 9:22; Matthew 16:24; 20:17-19). These verses show that Jesus himself spoke of His coming death by crucifixion and that His purpose in dying was to be a ransom for man to bring him back to fellowship with God.

3. Do you believe in the Trinity?

Many Muslims have heard that the word *trinity* is not found in the Bible. This helps support their idea that it is a made up doctrine. It, of course, seems to contradict the central theme of Islam—that Allah is one.

Exploration in the Place of Explanation

Here is a true story about how one believer dealt with the question of the Trinity directed to him by four Muslim men.

Jeff was doing some doctoral research and found it necessary to interview four men who were Muslims. As they sat in a restaurant drinking coffee, one of the four, whom we will call Ali, asked without warning, "Can you explain to me the Trinity?" Just like that, without warning the dreaded "T" question. Ali seemed to be well informed on both the Council of Nicea and the Creed by the same name. "So why should I believe in the Trinity?" he asked.

As he began to sip his coffee, Jeff thought about the kind of response he could give—there was the "God as one essence but still three distinct persons" approach. Then he could always fall back on the "mystery of the Godhead" method. But he knew Muslims would not understand any of these analogies, for they all break down under scrutiny. Their common question is how can 1+1+1 still equal one? We could suggest multiplication rather than addition, but it is still the same problem—analogies don't satisfy. Reverting to "It's a mystery" brings their refrain that Christians are irrational! Though Muslims believe God is unknowable, they forget that fact when they are asking Christians about the Trinity. Jeff finally realized that trying to define this doctrine would not work, **for philosophical discussion usually just leads to confusion.**

Setting down his coffee, he said, "The definition of the Trinity is not infallible; the word is not in the Scripture. Therefore, I refuse to speak about the definition!" Ali had no reply; he was speechless. His "T" bomb had suddenly lost its power. After a moment, Jeff said, "But can I tell you a story?" Since Jeff refused to discuss the Nicene Creed, Ali finally agreed. After all, everyone enjoys a good story.

"I am consistently amazed at the power of story," says Jeff. "Educated to think propositionally, I have been converted to the use of biblical stories in evangelism—especially with Muslims." What he proposes is that we should not try to *explain* God, or in this case the Trinity, but rather tell the stories that *describe* God. Explanation requires an expert and that can easily lead to an adversarial situation. Exploration or description, on the other hand, is driven by questions and not answers, and focuses on the story, not the expert. Explanations require definitions; exploration requires narrative. Explanations can take us out of the Scripture, such as the case with the Nicene Creed, but exploration is telling the story and enjoying the details, and allowing the Scripture to work. In addition, asking questions during the story will encourage Muslims to think through their own beliefs before they start to attack ours.

Ali, with the others, agreed to hear the story. What story should Jeff tell? What story would you tell if you were in his place? You might tell the story of Jesus' baptism where all three members of the Trinity were present. But might this still be an attempt to define the Trinity? Jeff began to tell the story in Genesis 2 and 3: God placing man in the Garden, creating the woman, God meeting with man and asking him questions, man's sin and eventually God providing the skins of animals to cover them. This relationship between God and man was his emphasis, because that is missing from the Quranic version of the story. When he finished, he just looked at the four men … no explanation, no conclusion, nothing! The Muslims should have been asking, "How can God talk to man? How is He running the universe at the same time? Why slay animals to cover the first couple's nakedness?" These questions may not have initially helped them better understand the triune God. Yet, the process would begin for them to **understand the Trinity is a relationship, not just a definition!** Sharing Bible stories allow Muslims to explore the way in which God has revealed himself.

Three of the four men were satisfied with the answer; they just wanted to understand the details. But Ali still had a question. He wanted to know about the Nicene Creed due to its Middle Eastern origin (rather than European or American). Jeff then did something that Jesus might have done in such a case. He offered to answer the question, if Ali would answer his question first. Everyone was listening. Jeff asked, "Is the Quran the created or the uncreated word of Allah! If it is uncreated, how do you explain the existence of two uncreated entities, Allah and his word?" Ali started to answer, but Jeff continued, "In my opinion, if Muslims have two uncreated entities, they have the same problem as Christians, who just have three." Just as 1+1+1 can't equal 1, so 1+1 can't be 1 either. Ali had an answer, but it was not a story. Finally he said it is a mystery, for he admitted that the Quran was uncreated. The analogy of the two beliefs answered his question. Jeff believes that stories and questions can be a great source of materials for Muslim evangelism. Tough questions can be answered with stories, metaphors, analogies and tough questions. When we deal with the hard questions of the faith, the answer is usually a good story!

CHANGING THE ENVIRONMENT

Folk Islam

It is important to know that most Muslims in the world are not devout. They are nominal Muslims who tend to be lax in their religious duties and go to the mosque only on Fridays or holidays. Many of them are still religious, but the Islam they adhere to reveals to us an entirely different side of their faith—the dark side—which we commonly refer to as Folk Islam, the religion of the people. It's a religion that features good spirits and evil spirits, white magic and black magic, the evil eye, amulets and charms, dreams and omens, fortune tellers and witchdoctors, Muslim saints and shrines.

At the heart of Folk Islam is the belief that, before Allah created the human race, he created a race of spirit beings, known as the *jinn*. These are said to be created from pure fire and possess supernatural power. In the beginning, all of these jinn were good jinn. However, when Allah created humankind, one of the jinn became envious and rebelled against him. Allah cursed him, and this cursed jinn and his followers vowed to terrorize the human race until the end of time. That *jinn* became known as *Ash-Shaitan*, "The Rebel." For Muslims, this event marked the beginning of evil and the origin of Satan and his evil cohorts. According to Islamic teaching, there are now both good jinn and bad jinn who inhabit the earth with humans. Jinn can either help or torment people.

Most Muslims are dreadfully fearful of the jinn, which is

why they have a variety of daily customs to provide special protection. For example, Muslims speak or display sacred Arabic words and the names of Allah that are believed to be infused with power to ward off the jinn. Muslims also use certain verses from the Quran which are believed to possess special powers of protection. Another common practice is burning sweet-smelling incense inside the home. According to Muslim tradition, the evil jinn are attracted to bad smells, thus Muslims conversely believe they are repelled by good smells.

Some Muslims even try to use trickery. For example, Muslims believe that babies and small children are especially vulnerable to the jinn, so mothers will call their children by nicknames to conceal their true identities. And because they believe that the jinn specifically target baby boys, mothers will dress their little boys to look like girls in order to confuse the jinn.

Whenever Muslims feel that they face grave danger or believe they have already been attacked by jinn, they seek the services of professionals. These practitioners—known as *shamans, marabouts,* or *faqirs,* depending on their location in the Muslim world—are reputed to have special power over the jinn. Their expertise includes protection and cures against the jinn. Whatever their specialty, they enter the spirit realm through occult rituals that include fasting, ablution, incantation, and even drugs. It is in the altered state of consciousness that they supposedly become empowered to prepare amulets and charms which are then worn by the client on the body or clothing, or placed somewhere in the home.

In addition to these local spirit practitioners, Islamic history identifies certain individuals who became widely celebrated for their religious teaching, charisma, and extraordinary miracles, such as walking on water or healing the sick. These individuals were believed to possess special power to bestow upon their followers divine blessings called *baraka*. When these individuals died, their followers elevated them to sainthood and transformed their tombs into elaborate shrines. Muslims believe the saint's spirit resides at his shrine, ready always to bestow blessing.

Muslims by the thousands flock to shrines and spirit practitioners in hope of some miracle to help them in their time of crisis. A wife may be barren; a child may be fatally ill or demon-possessed. A businessman may be worried about a future transaction; a woman may suspect a husband of infidelity. A government official may suspect a curse has been placed upon him by a political rival. **Orthodox Islam has no answer for these kinds of pressing problems except to fully submit to whatever fate Allah has decreed.** Most people are not ready to simply submit to their difficulty. They want to rise above it, to exert some measure of control over their fate. They want to find a source of power that can change their situation for the perceived good. Furthermore, their hearts yearn for a mediator to act on their behalf. Those they seek have a special connection to Allah, they believe, and they look to him for intercession and special favors. Shrines are especially frequented by Muslim women, since they are usually discouraged from attending the mosque, but are free to visit the shrine. This is one place where Muslim women can seek to fulfill their desire for some spiritual connection and some sense of self-worth.

Need of a Mediator

We draw two very important lessons from our understanding of Folk Islam. First, many Muslims sense a dire need for a mediator, an intercessor. This yearning reflects one of the deepest cries of the heart. It is echoed in one of the oldest books of the Bible—Job (9:32-34): "For he [God] is not a man, as I am, that I might answer him, that we should come to trial together. There is no arbiter between us who might lay his hand on us both. Let him take his rod away from me, and let not dread of him terrify me." This is the epitome of the universal plea for a mediator between God and man, and it is so prevalent in the Muslim world.

Need for Power

Second, we learn that Muslims constantly feel the need for a source of power to deliver them from evil. But the teaching of the Quran, which has led Muslims to believe that there are good spirits and evil spirits on earth that can be tamed for the good of humankind, is a falsehood. It is a deception that has misled millions of Muslims. It has propelled them into a realm of counterfeit spiritual powers and counterfeit deliverers. It has lured them into the snare of witchcraft—which offers an apparent temporary cure, but ultimately produces a life of dependency and fear. According to the Bible, the only spirits that dwell here on earth are fallen angels and only evil. Not one of them is good. And there is no such thing as white magic. The objective of these evil spirits is to harm people and corrupt their souls—to lead them to eternal damnation. (Read, remember and reinforce the following with your Muslim friend: Leviticus 19:26-28, 31; Isaiah 8:19; Acts 16:16; Exodus 22:18; Acts 19:19; Leviticus 20:6.)

We already know that "the god of this world has blinded the minds of the unbelievers, to keep them from seeing the light of the gospel of the glory of Christ..." (2 Corinthians 4:4). Add the element of witchcraft and the plight of Muslims seems even more dire. Because of witchcraft, most Muslims are likely to be open to the spirit realm. Westerners usually label as superstition such things as supernatural signs, dreams and visions.

It is critical for believers to realize that when we step into the territory of Islam, we need to be prepared to meet up with spiritual forces that defy the gospel. We need to be prepared to confront spirit beings and counterfeit powers that are hostile to God. We need to be filled and empowered by the Holy Spirit as were those in the Book of Acts. We must be prepared for spiritual warfare, where we can see the Light dispel the Darkness and set the captives free. Prayer is crucial. Notice how the disciples prayed and how God responded:

> "And now Lord, look upon their threats and grant to your servants to continue to speak your word with all boldness, while you stretch out your hand to heal, and signs and wonders are performed through the name of your holy servant Jesus." And when they had prayed, the place in which they were gathered together was shaken, and they were all filled with the Holy Spirit and continued to speak the word of God with boldness. (Acts 4:29-31)

God still uses signs and wonders today to confirm who Jesus is—the Savior of the world, the Mediator, in whose name there is forgiveness of sins. Muslims themselves bear witness to the fact that miracles in Jesus' name continue to transform lives. The following is one such testimony:

"I believed in Allah, a god who doesn't do anything for me. He is not alive and I could not have a relationship with him. I was empty inside with no peace or joy. I did have a good family and they did care about me. Yet, I was so empty. The process of me coming to know Christ as Savior is really a miracle. I miscarried during my first pregnancy. The second pregnancy everything was okay. However, after five months during the third pregnancy, I began to bleed. I lost the baby in the hospital.

"I was angry with Allah. I was sad and depressed. I wanted to commit suicide. My husband tried to help, but I shut the door on assistance. I then experienced my fourth pregnancy. But, I started to bleed again. During this time I met a Christian lady. She challenged me to ask God to show me the truth. So one night I knelt and prayed for God to show me the truth. I was really wanting Him to change my heart and life situations. A miracle happened. I stopped bleeding. The doctors were amazed that the placenta was no longer in detachment. I visited the Christian lady and she shared the message of Christ's work. I did not know that God, but I wanted to experience Him. I prayed a simple prayer and joy flooded my soul. Jesus changed me completely."

We are reminded of Jesus' words to the apostle Paul in Acts 26:17-18: "I am sending you to open their eyes, so that they may turn from darkness to light and from the power of Satan to God, that they may receive forgiveness of sins and a place among those who are sanctified by faith in me."

In the same way, the Lord may send you to a Muslim friend or neighbor to lovingly turn him or her from the power of Satan to the power of God. You may be the one whom God will use to lead a Muslim to such a miracle—a miracle of divine power and radical transformation!

"POWER ENCOUNTERS" AMONG MUSLIMS

Today the Western world is entangled with ideas based on materialism and humanism. When the Christian witness presents biblical truths to Muslims, there ensues a power confrontation or "encounter" of opposing forces. Nothing less than the Holy Spirit-anointed message of the "full gospel" will be effective. As Tim Warner explains it:

"Power encounter is the demonstration by God's servants of God's 'incomparably great power for us who believe' (Ephesians 1:19) based on the work of Christ on the Cross (Colossians 2:15) and the ministry of the Holy Spirit (Acts 1:8) in confrontation with and victory over the work of Satan and demons (Luke 10:19) in their attacks on God's children or their control of unbelievers resulting in the glory of God and salvation of the lost and/or the up building of believers."[3]

Further, a power encounter is an open, public confrontation between opposing spiritual forces. In Muslim evangelism, the power on one side is the Spirit of God acting through the Christian witness who proclaims Christ. On the other side, there are unregenerated hearts of people along with the spiritual forces of evil in opposition. The latter forces act through Islamic beliefs and traditions backed by religious, political, and social authorities. The evil forces instigate bitter conflict by spreading hatred and animosity and by keeping people blind to the truth.

In a narrow sense, power encounter is an internal debate in the mind and heart of a person, whether to accept Christ or remain loyal to Islam, as the Holy Spirit woos the person. The power encounter includes a tangible demonstration of the superiority of Christ. In other words, there is a primary and subtle encounter in the minds of Muslims who are being evangelized as they compare Islam and Christianity. When Christ is offered to a Muslim, Satan tries to keep a tight grip on that person. Intense spiritual warfare for this soul begins. Christ has promised: "I have given you authority ... over all the power of the enemy" (Luke 10:19).

Demonstrations of God's power to meet people's felt needs in the name of Jesus are important catalysts to hinder hostility toward the gospel. The Scriptures provide us with a solid foundation for power encounters. The Word says that speaking in tongues is a sign for unbelievers. "Thus tongues," writes Paul, "are a sign not for believers but for unbelievers" (1 Corinthians 14:22). Sometimes signs and wonders, in addition to speaking in tongues, are needed to inspire faith. As the disciples preached the message of salvation, God "worked with them and confirmed his word by the signs that accompanied it" (Mark 16:20, NIV). Paul reminded the church at Corinth, "My message and my preaching were not with wise and persuasive words, but with a demonstration of the Spirit's power" (1 Corinthians 2:4, NIV). The Greek word translated here as "demonstration" literally means "proof"—something that is forceful enough to bring conviction.

Preaching Christ in the power of the Holy Spirit gets Muslims' attention and confirms Christ's claims. Sobhi Malek, in an address given at the Assemblies of God Consultation in Baguio City, Philippines (Feb. 2005), said: "I know of Muslims who came to Christ because of the work of the gifts of the Spirit. Fadhila was attracted to the church because people there spoke in tongues! And even before she accepted the Lord in her life, she expressed her amazement at such a miracle and once she said to me: 'To speak in a language that you never learned is really a witness that God is in you!' Today she is a strong believer and is baptized in the Holy Spirit."

The system of Islam will continue to have the upper hand in the hearts and minds of Muslims unless they are confronted with the power of the resurrected Christ. The power of the gospel as demonstrated by mighty acts of the Holy Spirit is often required to break the bondage of generations of belief in Islam.

The first reason for power encounter is the folk Islamic worldview. To initiate such an encounter when ministering to Muslims involved in folk practices is most appropriate. In the Bible, such confrontation of forces often gave servants of God an open door to speak for Him and declare His glory (1 Kings 18:36-39; Acts 28:3-10). These acts also motivated people to listen to the message (Acts 8:6-7). Likewise, in Muslim evangelism, when there is a power encounter, when people see the glory of God at work and hear the message of the gospel, the Holy Spirit will minister to needs, cast out evil spirits, heal sick and suffering bodies, dispel fears about the future, grant security and assurance, and fill hearts with Christ's love.

The Muslim perspective of power is also influenced by the concept of *jihad*, or holy war. One definition of jihad is the religious duty that Muslims must answer when war is being waged against non-Muslims (Quran 9:5). They respect power. For them, nonviolence is not a virtue; rather, it is despicable. To turn the other cheek, in their eyes, means to acknowledge defeat. To be unified, powerful, and victorious are signs of Allah's approval. Their respect for power allows the Christian witness to find an open door to minister. Christ is mightier than the jinn and spirits; and sickness and disease can be cured in His name. Spiritual victories are possible in the name of Jesus. A demonstration of power will command their attention.

A BIBLICAL PERSPECTIVE

The proclamation of the kingdom of God will always induce a confrontation of forces. The apostle Paul characterizes the kingdom of God as more than mere talk—it is a matter of power (1 Corinthians 4:20). Divine power is a sign of the presence of the kingdom of God. Since the kingdom of God is the rule of the King over the universe and people's hearts, its proclamation induces an ongoing spiritual battle. This conflict is between God's kingdom and the temporary rule of Satan, who is assisted by demonic forces under his command. This is illustrated in 1 Samuel 5 and 6, the account of the Ark of the Covenant among the Philistines. The Philistines had captured the Ark and brought it to Ashdod. To demonstrate the power of their false god, Dagon, they placed the Ark beside the Dagon image. The next morning the people of Ashdod found Dagon had fallen face down before the Ark of the Lord. The Lord troubled the people of Ashdod and its surrounding towns, causing devastation and afflicting them with tumors. Only when they offered gifts of gold and gave glory to the God of Israel did His anger and wrath lift.

HOW DOES POWER ENCOUNTER WORK?

There are two types of power encounter. In the first, the Christian takes the initiative and attacks Satan's domain. Here, Satan finds himself on the defensive. In the second, Satan initiates the attack against the kingdom of God; in turn the Christian has to stand firm in Christ against the enemy.

Divine healing and exorcism are common areas of engagement. If there is sickness and the Lord reveals that it is due to demonic forces, it is our duty to pray for the sick and rebuke those powers in the name of Jesus. If a person is demonized, it is our duty to cast out the demons in Christ's name.

Another area where power encounter can advance God's cause is through a confession of faith evoked with the use of questions. The form of the confession should be declarative: "Yes, I believe." Rather than asking a Muslim convert to recite a creedal statement, ask questions that require a new believer to say, "Yes, I believe." With each such response the believer is emerging triumphant from an encounter in which Jesus' name is glorified.

In Muslim evangelism the Church faces spiritual warfare on a tremendous scale. Nothing less than the power of the Holy Spirit and the Word of the gospel will be able to defeat these forces. The gospel brings with it healing for the sick, deliverance for the demonized, and victory in the name of Jesus.[4]

DREAMS AND VISIONS

In the recent past God has worked among Muslims in an increasingly supernatural way. Muslims are having dreams and visions of Jesus. This has led many of them to seek out the people who say that "Jesus is the Son of God." These Christian neighbors and associates are known as followers of Jesus. Muslims believe that Allah still communicates with people through dreams and visions. Let's discuss this further.

Biblical Background

The Bible is full of examples of believers who were led and directed at critical moments by dreams and visions. Most of the Old Testament was written by prophets of God to whom the Lord had spoken directly. Joseph, son of Jacob, had numerous dreams as preparation for moving his family from Canaan to Egypt so they would not suffer starvation. Though God spoke in dreams and visions to the prophets of Israel, He spoke to Moses face to face (Numbers 12:6-8).

Unbelievers saw visions too. The first clear record of this was Abimelech concerning his treatment of Abraham and Sarah (Genesis 20:3; Genesis 12 may imply that Pharaoh of Egypt had such a dream). Daniel was led to interpret the dreams of pagan kings while in exile (Daniel 2, 4, 5), and Pilate's wife told of the frightful dream she had just before the trial of Jesus (Matthew 27:19). There is the great story of Saul who became Paul the apostle (Acts 9). This was such a powerful experience that Luke refers to it later in the same book (Acts 22, 26). Many dreams and visions are still part of the plan of our supernatural God, to draw men and women to faith.

Examples from Our Day

In a religion where Allah is supposed to be unknowable and distant, having a significant dream or meeting someone wearing a glowing white robe is an "attention grabber" of the first order. There appears to be a general pattern to these events in Muslim lives today:

- The Muslim will encounter some event or need in their life that presents a pressing problem they cannot solve. In missions we call this a "felt need." The person seeking a solution wants help with the situation. They seek out someone they believe has "power" in the spirit world. This might even involve meeting with a Christian through an unexpected series of circumstances.

- As these Muslims seek God, they experience a dream or vision about heaven, hell, or their personal future. In this visitation a man in a glowing white robe appears, usually identified by them as Jesus. In most visions they understand who He is without being told. He usually speaks few words, such as "Follow Me," "Read My Word," or "I love you." He gives them specific instructions that must be followed. Those instructions usually lead them to a believer who will share the gospel with them or give them a Bible. The intent is to get them exposed to the truth—God's Word—which they may have never heard or accepted. This divine encounter totally changes the direction of their lives.

- They respond to the vision or the dream by seeking out a true disciple of Jesus who will answer their questions and deliver the truth to them. Jesus never explains the plan of salvation, but leaves it up to a disciple to explain God's will to the Muslim who is seeking truth. Later they face the fires of persecution but also usually find some means of meeting with other believers for encouragement. As they grow, they also become witnesses. They seek out others whom they pray for and believe with for their own felt needs … and the cycle starts again.

THE POWER OF PENTECOST

If we break through into the personal world of Muslims, it will require an anointing and power from God. Then we can speak and act in a way that will destroy the blindness and bondage they experience. As Spirit-directed people, God wants us to work with Him. As it was for the Early Church in Acts, God's will for us today is to be bold, fearing neither men nor demons. When God speaks in a still, small voice, He will direct us to pray for the sick, for the demonized, and for miracles beyond our comprehension. We still serve a God who desires and wills to supernaturally reveal His power to those who are lost.

CONCLUSION

Power encounters seem to have been lost to many in ministry—even among those who call themselves Pentecostal. Power encounter is like a new realization for the Church in our day, as was the power of Pentecost in the recent past. We have only scratched the surface of this important topic, and there is much more to be learned. We encourage you to read more on this important topic. There are a number of good books written on the subject. (See a partial suggested list below.) Then realize that to be a good disciple involved in ministry, you will need to see power encounter as part of your work for our Lord. You will want to trust the Lord, take a risk, be willing to learn, and pray as never before. You will be used to build up the kingdom of Christ by listening and obeying the leadings of the Holy Spirit. Don't be afraid to discuss this topic with other believers and ask the Lord to help you learn by leading you to others who have seen power encounters in their ministries. Lastly, expect God to work! Be looking for Muslims to have dreams, visions, and supernatural encounters. Be expectant.

Prayer Points:

- Pray that you will always minister in the power of the Holy Spirit as you recognize the spiritual forces your Muslim friend is encountering.

- Pray that you will have boldness to believe that greater is He that is in you than he that is in the world.

- Pray that your Muslim friend will have a supernatural encounter with Jesus.

Action Steps:

- Ask your Muslim friend, "Do you believe in spiritual encounters?"

- Review the Book of Acts. Take note of the "power encounters" that are recorded.

- Read good books on the subject of power encounter and ministry in the power of the Holy Spirit. We recommend:

Dempster, M.A., B.D. Klaus, and D. Petersen. *Called and Empowered: Global Mission in Pentecostal Perspective.* Peabody, MA: Hendrickson Publishers, 1991.

Horton, Stanley. *What the Bible Says about the Holy Spirit.* Springfield, MO: Gospel Publishing House, 1976.

Miller, Denzil. *Power Encounter: Ministering in the Power and Anointing of the Holy Spirit.* Springfield, MO: PneumaLife Publications, 2013; www.decadeofpentecost.org.

Reddin, Opal, Ed. *Power Encounter: A Pentecostal Perspective: Demons in Believers? Territorial Spirits? Generational Curses? Binding and Loosing?* Springfield, MO: Central Bible College Press, 1999.

Review Questions:

1. How does "Folk Islam" differ from orthodox Islam that would be practiced by devout Muslims?

2. What two basic human needs does Folk Islam reveal?

3. As Bible-believing Christians, what do we mean by the term "power encounter"?

4. Describe an example of how God could use a dream or vision to bring Muslims into a salvation experience.

5. How does the Pentecostal experience give Christians an advantage in their effort to lead Muslims to the lordship of Christ?

NOTES

NOTES

NOTES

NOTES

OUTREACH TO MUSLIMS: CREATING A NEW ENVIRONMENT

The objective for Lesson 4 is:

That you would create/seize opportunities
to befriend and witness to Muslims.

CHAPTER SUMMARY

In this lesson we look at actions or lifestyles that impact the witness to Muslims. What can we do to create an interacting environment between Muslims and Christians? We will explore cultural understandings and misunderstandings, points of conversations and look at the questions that Muslims have because of their faith. We will explore specific points of additional "felt-needs" in Muslim lives that can offer an opportunity for a relationship to develop which can then lead to a powerful witness.

Testimony

Carl Ellis in answering the question "What are some practical things to know as we reach out to black Muslims with the gospel?" stated, "There are three things that a Muslim, a Hindu, or anybody else has no resistance against: the prayer of the saints, the love of the saints, and the wise application of biblical truth to their core issues—whatever those issues are. Every Muslim that I've met who came to Christ always came to Christ for one of those reasons, and the one that I hear mentioned mostly is the love."[5]

CHAPTER OUTLINE

Overcoming Fear to Befriend

Need of the Messenger to Be Intentional

    Be a Learner

    Time

    Ability to Communicate

Overcoming Misunderstandings

Cultural Understandings: Behavior and Practices That Build Bridges

    Mannerisms and Attitude to Create an Appropriate Atmosphere for Witness

As Friendships Develop, Muslims Ask

    Has the Bible been changed and is therefore not trustworthy?

    A Testimony

    Questions Regarding Muslims' Felt/Spiritual Needs

Possible Questions to Ask Muslims

Opportunities to Connect with Muslims

Guidelines for Conversation

Conclusion

    Testimony

    Prayer Points

    Action Steps

    Review Questions

OVERCOMING FEAR TO BEFRIEND

Making a Muslim friend is not as hard as it might seem. Apprehensions—on both sides—make the process more difficult. Muslims can be afraid of us because they see themselves as a minority in "Christian" America. Remember, they believe *everyone* who lives in the West is a Christian. Fear of the unknown more than anything else separates Muslims and Christians.

Christians should realize the ultimate source of fear is the enemy of our souls, Satan. Since the work we want to engage in has as its end result the destruction of his kingdom, we can readily see why he opposes us. Fear also comes due to lack of faith and trust. If the thought of speaking to Muslims brings you fear, know that you are not alone.

Jesus told the disciples to not be afraid, because He said, "I have overcome the world" (John 16:33). Before He left this world, and before the disciples were left to spread the Good News, Jesus promised two things. First, He said, "I am with you always, even to the end of the age" (Matthew 28:20, NKJV). What did He promise? Nothing less than His presence, and that should be sufficient for us. Second, He promised us the Holy Spirit would come to guide and comfort us. He is called both the Counselor and the Comforter, depending on the translation, in John, chapters 14-16. Both meanings should calm our fears. He did not promise the disciples that they would always be safe and secure. In fact, we are told that all who "live godly in Christ Jesus shall suffer persecution" (2 Timothy 3:12, KJV). With the persecution, Jesus promised that what we should say would be given to us directly from the Holy Spirit (Mark 13:11). So we have the promise of His presence and His power! So how do we get to know Muslims?

The first requirement for evangelism with an individual Muslim is to know a Muslim, because evangelism with

Muslims must be relational. It is not "hit and run" where we simply communicate and then leave, assuming the person will understand the message. It is the delivery of your life to the life of a Muslim. This is what Jesus did when He came to earth. He delivered God himself, packaged as a man, and we can do no less!

NEED OF THE MESSENGER TO BE INTENTIONAL

To reach Muslims requires that they become a priority to us. This ministry is not easy. We are easily diverted to other things that are less confrontational and appear capable of producing more results. A simple wave and greeting will not open the heart of a Muslim to Christ or give you the opportunity to share your witness. You must create space in your life for a Muslim friend, associate, or neighbor. It may require adjustments in your life to make a Muslim feel comfortable. If you invite them to your home, you may need to be prepared to live more simply, dress in a more conservative fashion, and turn off the TV and other electronics. For Muslims to hear we will probably need to slow down our busy pace of life.

Be a Learner

To communicate effectively, we must determine to become continual learners about the people we desire to introduce to Jesus. Even if you understand the basic doctrines and practices of Islam, even if you have read the Quran, the Muslim's faith remains complex. Muslim people range from very orthodox to very liberal. The important questions you need to find answers for are: Who is your Muslim friend? Where does he or she fit in their own complex world? You discover this by listening carefully and asking sensitive questions. There is one constant, however. It will always be the same. Before anything else, *this person is a Muslim; their first and strongest loyalty is to Islam.*

Time

In the West people say, "Time is money." What they often mean by this is, "My time is too valuable to waste it on speaking to a person like you!" The Muslim can say almost the same thing, with a nearly opposite meaning, as in, "Time is the most valuable thing I have to give you, and I will share it to show you how much I value and honor you." To truly get to know a Muslim friend will take time and effort, and sometimes even money. But remember, this is also an investment in eternity, made worthwhile when the Muslim begins to ask sincerely about your faith in Christ.

Ability to Communicate

The ability to communicate with your audience is vital, but what does communication really include? Muslims may want to learn to speak English, or, more likely, *better* English. Are you willing to learn some of their language at the same time? What are the interests of the family? Are they religious people, or do they seem more interested in sports? Do they like movies or just sit around and tell stories? Are they interested in American family life and how we raise our children or are they concerned that their own children in this new country maintain their own traditions?

Jesus himself asked many questions of the people who came to Him. It is important that we communicate our personal concern for them. How will we communicate the love of God for them, when they believe for the most part that God does not love? When we communicate with them, what do we hope to accomplish?

OVERCOMING MISUNDERSTANDINGS

As you approach Muslim people, first see them simply as human beings. Meet them as neighbors before you see them as Muslims or announce that you're a Christian.[6] Can you make friends with someone in a school, around the local mosque, or in the marketplace? If you already know a Muslim, an acquaintance, perhaps you should ask how you can deepen that relationship and make it more meaningful. Words like these can help: "I am so glad to meet you. I would really like to know more about your way of life. If there is anything I can do to help you, please let me know, even now." Avoid personal questions at first. **Take time to listen and build trust.** If you have sought them out, they will want to know who you are, your occupation and what your values are.

Consider the example of Jesus in Luke 2:46-47. Here Jesus is meeting with the religious leaders in Jerusalem at the age of 12. Notice that He was *sitting* with the leaders. As He sat, He *listened*, and only then did He ask *questions*. His questions would not have been to trip them up, but to engage them in real dialogue. What impressed these leaders is that Jesus not only had knowledge of the facts, but He also demonstrated an understanding of them. All three of these behaviors can help in starting a dialogue with a Muslim neighbor or friend—being with them, listening to their words, and asking questions.[7]

In America the habit of hospitality has been largely lost because of the busyness of life. In the East, hospitality remains a sacred duty to perform for all who come to visit one's home (usually unannounced). When should visits be made? You can visit for any event of joy or sorrow when people want or need fellowship. Hospitality is also a way to say thank you or I am sorry for what happened to my neighbor.

CULTURAL UNDERSTANDINGS: BEHAVIOR AND PRACTICES THAT BUILD BRIDGES

If the Holy Spirit is prodding you to reach out in love to a Muslim you have met or know of, be ready to take action. If you are not sure where to begin, first and foremost, begin with prayer. Ask the Holy Spirit for guidance and discernment. Pray for an open door. Pray for the right time and the right place. Make it your objective to befriend these Muslims and to be a blessing. Your mission is to establish an enduring relationship that will ultimately attract them to Jesus within you.

If your "bridge building" is to African-American Muslims, remember that cultural and economic empowerment are major concerns. Their core cultural issues are:

- Identity
- Dignity
- Divine global significance
- Pain
- Rage
- A quest for masculinity[8]

Your awareness of and manner of dealing with these issues directly impacts your ability to lead your Muslim friends to Jesus.

Mannerisms and Attitude to Create an Appropriate Atmosphere for Witness

The guiding principle should be: "Have this attitude in yourselves which was also in Christ Jesus" (Philippians 2:5, NASB).

DO:

- Pray! Intercessory prayer for Muslims will soften your heart toward them and soften their hearts toward the gospel.

- SHARE YOUR PERSONAL TESTIMONY!

- Try to put yourself in their place.

- Build long-term relationships with Muslims; they must see your consistent Christian life.

- Respect Muslims.

- Love Muslims; they must feel the "warmth" of Christian love.

- Show them you care about them as persons, not just their souls.

- Be willing to give a significant amount of time to one individual.

- Start with values you have in common with Muslims.

- Show them hospitality.

- Give your Muslim friend a Bible, a New Testament, or one of the Gospels.

- Use the Word of God whether he/she believes the Bible or not (Hebrews 4:12-13).

- Pray together.

- Encourage the Muslim to believe with you for a miracle from God.

- Ask your Muslim friend if they have had any significant dreams.

- Give the seeker time to reflect, understand, and count the cost. They must desire conversion.

- Tug at, or appeal to, their heart (emotions).

- Help Muslims process questions, doubts and confusion they may have about the Islamic faith. This is best accomplished through patient listening, calm discussion, and encouraging them that God will lead them into truth if they seek Him with all their hearts.

DO NOT:

- Do not consider Muslims as your enemies.

- Do not insult Muhammad, the Quran, or Muslim people.

- Do not argue (debate), but rather witness and use reason.

- Do not pressure a Muslim to confess a premature decision.

- Do not be afraid to say, "I don't know."

- Do not make it your practice to witness to the opposite sex. Men should witness to men; women should witness to women.

- Do not ask Muslims if they want to go to heaven (Paradise) unless you explain that heaven is where God is.

After you have prayed, have the courage to knock on their door and introduce yourself. If they are new immigrants, settling in from overseas, offer to help them. You can direct them, or even take them, to various social services that specialize in employment, education, and health care. If they're struggling with English, you can help them fill out complicated forms. If, however, they are American born or converts to Islam you can simply start by saying, "Hello."

When you go to their door to introduce yourself, take along a gift item—preferably a fruit basket. Be careful about taking homemade food, such as bakery items. Muslims are suspicious of food that might contain pork fat (lard). Include a personal note along with your name and telephone number. The note could read something like this: "Welcome to our community. May God bless you and your family." Most likely, the Muslim will feel obligated to invite you inside his home. However, because you caught him off guard, find an excuse to politely refuse. Then, make a point to call him about a future visit.

As you continue to build on the relationship you have started, it won't take long to notice the enthusiasm Muslims have for hospitality. This aspect of Islamic culture helps us to better understand the words of Jesus in Revelation 3:20: "Behold, I stand at the door and knock. If anyone hears my voice and opens the door, I will come in to him and eat with him, and he with me." Eating together is a sign of mutual acceptance. Have no doubt that you will be invited by Muslims as a guest into their home. Out of courtesy, your Muslim host will treat you like royalty and set before you the best he has. If you are with a spouse, both of you will be seated at the same table and left to eat together. Your host family members will look on, ready and eager to serve. Unless you are familiar with Muslim etiquette, despite your verbal pleas, they will keep your plates heaped with food and supply you with one bottle of cola after another.

As you continue to interact with your Muslim friends, you will learn the gestures and words that say, "Thank you, I have eaten enough food and am pleasantly satisfied." You will hear them say *bismillah* (in the name of Allah) at the onset of the meal and *alhamdulillah* (praise be to Allah) at the end. You will want to remember the significance of eating only with your right hand, never with the left one (the left hand is understood to be the hand that cleans the body). You will learn the practice of sipping a glass of water after your meal to rinse your mouth. Though you may be served together at the same table in the Muslims' home, you will learn that ordinarily, when there are guests, men eat in one room, and the women eat in another room (unless they are relatives). And throughout the visit, the men and women remain segregated.

If you want this Muslim family to reciprocate your visit by coming to your home, you will need to continue to respect their social norms on your own turf. Remember, Muslim hospitality means guests are highly honored. During this first visit to your home, plan for a two- or three-course meal. Be careful not to include pork on the menu; it is strictly forbidden in Islam. Try to display enough food so that your guests never feel as though they are taking the last serving. That would imply that you did not consider them worthy of ample food. You must be the one to heap their plates until they have insisted that they have had enough. For many Muslim families, hospitality is a great sacrifice, but it is a sacrifice that can reap benefits. This is equally true for the Christian who learns how to properly and generously host Muslim guests.

As you and your family commit yourselves to getting to know a Muslim family, acquaintance, or coworker, you will likely begin to feel overwhelmed about possible cultural conflict. That's when you must ask yourself, *What would Jesus do?*

Jesus mingled with the people and became one of them. He spoke their language and ate their food. He socialized with them and prayed with them. He rejoiced and mourned with them. He made himself approachable and accessible. We now have the opportunity to continue this incarnational approach.

AS FRIENDSHIPS DEVELOP, MUSLIMS ASK

Has the Bible been changed and is therefore not trustworthy?

For most Muslims, this is a question answered in the affirmative because that is their only explanation for some of the differences between the Bible and the Quran. You could answer this question by pointing to all the textual evidence that we have for our present Scripture, but you will quickly lose their interest. A better approach would be to ask three simple questions about this issue (supported by follow-up questions) and let the honest inquirer answer for himself.

Question 1: "Who changed the Bible?" Was it the Jews or the Christians? Both peoples have had the Bible for at least 2,000 years. If the Jews changed it, why would the Christians accept those changes? And if it was the Christians, why should the Jews accept it? Both Jews and Christians were divided into several different sects. Which group changed the text (the answer is not important)? Why would the other groups accept such change? And in which language was it changed? The Bible was already in several different languages by the seventh century—Muhammad's time—including Coptic, Syriac, Latin, and French, to name a few. Another follow-up question would be, "How is it that all these languages have the *same* changes?"

The really difficult question is this: "Who is the real author of the Bible and is He not able to preserve it unchanged?" The answer here should be "yes," God is the author and He should be able to preserve it, or He is not a very strong God. To secure this answer you could make reference to these words of Jesus: "For truly, I say to you, until heaven and earth pass away, not an iota, not a dot, will pass from the Law until all is accomplished" (Matthew 5:18). "Heaven and earth will pass away, but my words will not pass away" (Matthew 24:35). And point to this psalm: "Forever, O Lord, your word is firmly fixed in the heavens" (Psalm 119:89).

Question 2: "When was the Bible changed?"

A Testimony

"David and I were rooming together. David pulled out a Bible. I said to him, 'David, you do know that the Bible has been changed, that the Bible has been tampered with. It's not the same Bible that was revealed to Christ hundreds of years ago.' He was ready for the question—far more ready than I anticipated. He said, 'We can test how much it has been changed through a science called textual criticism.' I began to look into it and I found out that the Bible hasn't really been changed all that much.... I began to realize, in fact, that no doctrine of the Bible has ever been changed.... A few years later, I began to realize that maybe I was wrong. It took quite a few years of debating this and researching this ... about three and a half years to come to this point to realize the Bible was true."

Unknown to many Muslims is the fact that Muhammad, in the first part of his "ministry," praised portions of "The Book" (our Bible) in the Quran on several occasions, including:

- The Quran instructs Muslims to believe "The Book" and threatens those who do not. Surah 2:121, 3:84, 10:94.

- The Quran says "The Book" gives direction, guidance and light for those who obey it. Surah 3:3, 5:44, 6:91.

- It states that "The Book" came from Allah. Surah 2:87, 5:46, 29:46.

The expanded question becomes then, "Was the change made before or after Muhammad's death?" If it was before, why does the Quran praise the Bible? And how could it be after Muhammad since we have thousands of copies of the Bible from before his time that say the same things as our present Bible.

Question 3: This is perhaps the most penetrating of all. "If the Jews and, especially, the Christians know their Scriptures have been changed, then why do millions of people continue to believe in them, and even willingly lay down their lives as martyrs?"

Questions Regarding Muslims' Felt/Spiritual Needs

This series of questions and answers was developed to help Muslims look at the important spiritual issues they need to address. Such questioning of their religion is not usually encouraged. These are in no particular order. The comments that follow each question should help you develop the ideas that you want to get across, no matter how your friend responds.

- "Why/how did the world become so miserable?"

Here we want to talk about the Islamic view of sin and why, if man is basically good, there is so much turmoil in the world and in individual lives. You should know that there are two views of sin among Muslims. Adam's sin did not permanently change man's nature and therefore mankind is not "fallen." Adam just asked forgiveness, it was granted, and that was it. Second, for the average man on the street, sin is not primarily committed against Allah, but against other men and women. Therefore if a person does not get caught in the act of sin, they are not really a sinner. This unfortunately leads

to an idea that certain wrongs are not sin because they remain
unknown.

- "How can I change my life?"

One of the major doctrines of the Islamic faith is
that Allah has predetermined everything in our lives. This is
expressed by the Arabic word *maktub*, meaning "that which
is written." The amazing thing is that most Muslims spend
a lot of time trying to change their destiny. Here, we would
want to emphasize the idea of human responsibility for our
situation and the choices one makes in life. Here would
be a place to talk about the power of Christ to deliver and
transform a life.

- "Is Allah really on my side?"

This is a question many Muslims are not sure has a
positive answer, but they are not asking it out loud yet either.
You get a hint of it when Muslims admit that "we all trust
Allah" and pray that "*maybe* Allah will help us." Muslims
often feel trapped because they cannot say with confidence
that Allah is with them. All they can affirm is that they
must continue to work on their "Islam" (submission). This
underlying fear is due to a total lack of assurance in Islam.
The judgment day looms large for many of them and they
never know if they have done enough good works. Islam also
teaches that some were created specifically for the fires of
hell. In this case Muslims need to hear about the true nature
of God, that He is a loving Heavenly Father "not willing that
any should perish" and that peace with God is possible.

- "What can I do right now to tip the scales of judgment
  in my favor?"

This is a question most Muslims will not ask, because
they think they already have done the needed good works or

they think there is no way to know the answer. Therefore, they have to leave it up to Allah. A related question is, "What happens to us after death—at the judgment of Allah we must all face?" The story of Cornelius in Acts 10 could be used—a man who had done good works but was still lacking in one thing, faith in Jesus.

- "How can I find freedom from shame?" or "How can I break free from a bad habit in my life?"

It is a great fear in the mind of a Muslim that shame might come upon himself or his family. It is what one experiences when family, friends, and neighbors know the individual has done wrong. It happens when someone in the group converts to another religion or a family member is caught in recurring sins such as fornication, drug abuse or drunkenness. Shame is a terrible thing and can lead to the murder of the offending individual to remove the shame the group feels. Again, the answer is truly surrendering to God through Christ.

- "Why is my life difficult even though I practice my religion to the best of my ability?"

This is a question especially difficult for Muslims since they believe they should always be triumphant if they have been a good Muslim. The idea of suffering as a means of being perfected into what God wants in our life is foreign to Muslim theology. Here we need to again talk about how sin brought into the world all the evil events we see and broken relationships we experience. The answer is to be set free from our personal sin and wait with confidence that Jesus will finally transform the world by His coming.

POSSIBLE QUESTIONS TO ASK MUSLIMS

* Do you ever think about Allah?

* In your thinking, what is Allah like?

* Do you know Allah personally?

* Is it possible to know Allah?

* How do you practice your religion?

* What do you say in your prayers?

* Do you ever talk to Allah personally from your heart?

* Does Allah hear you when you pray?

* Does he care about you?

* Is Allah concerned with your problems?

* Has Allah answered any of your prayers?

* (If yes, can you give an example?)

* Have you ever had any dreams in which you believe Allah was speaking?

* Have any of your friends had dreams?

* Are you ever troubled by jinn?

* (If yes, what do you do when this happens?)

* Does the Mullah (Marabout) have control over jinn?

* Who has power over jinn?

* What is sin?

* Does all sin need to be paid for?

* Will you go to hell for your sins?

* What is hell like?

* Is hell forever?

* Do you have peace with Allah?

* Do you know if your sins are forgiven?

* What do you do about your sins?

* Do you feel shame when you have done something displeasing to Allah?

* Do you have any hope of seeing Allah?

* Will you ever be in Allah's presence?

* What is heaven (Paradise) like?

* Who will be accepted into Paradise?

* What do you think about Christians?

* What do you think about Jesus?

* What does the Quran say about Jesus?

* Did Jesus live a sinless life?

* Did He work miracles?

* Do you have a copy of the Injil?

* Would you like one?

* Do you desire the blessings of God in your life?

* What would you like most of all that God should do for you?

* Could I pray for you, just now?

OPPORTUNITIES TO CONNECT WITH MUSLIMS

There are myriads of ways to connect with Muslim people in your neighborhood. The key is to start communication with them and determine their individual needs. This may require careful and Spirit-led observation and eventually actually extending yourself to befriend them. Here are some suggestions for the process.

- *Women's Ministry*

For instance, *Say Hello* is the ministry of the Assemblies of God to reach out to Muslim women and children. The concept is simple. Christian women and children start the process by greeting their Muslim neighbors with a simple "Hello." This ministry provides a number of materials to help you get started in conversation with and prayer for potential Muslim friends. They may be contacted at www.sayhello.org.

- *Campus Ministry*

One of the largest groups of receptive Muslims in America today is found on university campuses. Chi Alpha is the Assemblies of God ministry to this constantly changing group. With over 400 campus groups, there is probably one near you, especially in larger urban areas. They may be contacted at www.chialpha.com.

- *Chaplaincy*

Unfortunately, Muslims are also in the penal system of our country. Many of these are African-Americans who have accepted Islam while in the justice system. Here is an audience that is often looking for new answers to their present difficulties. Contact assistance can be found at www.chaplaincy.ag.org.

- *Sports*

Young men especially are looking for friends through sports. Seek out Muslim boys who are looking to become a part of your sports activities and teams.

- *Other Felt Needs*

Lists of other felt needs Muslims have are many and varied. For a new immigrant they could include: English language learning, citizenship classes, medical needs, tutoring, computers, food preparation, transportation, etc. If you have a skill or interest in any of these areas, focusing on them can assist you in opening a Muslim's heart to the gospel.

GUIDELINES FOR CONVERSATION

These guidelines are based on the idea that our goal is not to be confrontational, but to seize opportunities to share. Thus, we will treat Muslim people with respect and kindness. The great commandment of Jesus is to love God and love our neighbor (Matthew 22:37-39). Muslims will know when you really care about them, and nothing less than real love will do. The most effective approach to Muslims is true sacrificial love. Does that sound like something Jesus has already done?

Don't start an argument.

The first guideline for conversation is to avoid arguments. The Word tells us specifically in 2 Timothy 2:23-24 that the Lord's servant must not argue or quarrel but be kind to everyone. Sometimes believers want to argue Muslims into the kingdom of God, as though justification comes through the best argument, not by faith. If the Muslim persists in an argumentative attitude, it may be best to defer the conversation, or de-escalate the tension through calmness or even the use of humor.

What we want to do is *dialogue* with our Muslim friend. It was not the habit of Jesus or the Early Church to use argument or debate in the modern sense. Neither a yelling match or a formal debate (where each side presents its arguments presided over by a judge followed by questions and answers) is recommended. The apostle Paul "disputed" with the Jews at Athens (Acts 17:17, KJV). This word's meaning in Greek is "to think about things from different perspectives,"[9] as in presenting an idea in a speech. It is best rendered as *reasoned* or *discussed*.

Resist the temptation to criticize their faith.

A Testimony:

After going through a period of searching and reading the Bible, Hormoz testified: "Jesus did not fit the profile of a prophet that I had in mind. He let people worship him. A prophet will never do that. He will say, 'Don't worship me, worship God.' ... I was struggling with Jesus. Is He really a prophet? Is He really the Savior of the world? What about Muhammad? What about the Quran? I just struggled for months.

"Because I couldn't make a decision, I decided to go sit in a church, just to see what they were saying. One week, the pastor said, 'If anyone has a question, just come ask me.' I came up and asked him, 'Is Muhammad a prophet of God?' He thought for a few seconds, then he said, 'Well, what's your next question?' I asked, 'Is the Quran the Word of God?' He asked, 'Well, what's your next question?' I asked, 'How about my grandma? She is a very sincere Muslim. Does Christianity teach that she goes to hell?' The pastor avoided answering his questions. Finally he said, 'I do know one thing. Faith is very simple. Do you believe you are a sinner? ... Do you believe God loves you? ... Do you believe you cannot reach God? ... Do you believe God loved you so much that He came after you?'"

Hormoz realized he could answer yes to all these questions. Then the pastor said, "These few things you believe, that's enough."

Hormoz recounts what happened next: "As soon as the pastor said, 'That's enough,' suddenly things became so clear." At that moment, he was changed. His heart was filled with God's peace, joy and love. He was on the journey that would lead to his conversion.

Try to remove theological misunderstandings.

All that Muhammad knew about Christianity came to him orally. As a result, he made several wrong conclusions about orthodox Christianity and conveyed these ideas to his followers. One idea was that followers of Jesus worship *three gods*. To counter this idea in conversation, it would be good to reaffirm what Jesus said about the unity of God, which is also the greatest belief of Islam. To show this to Muslims, you could read to them Mark 12:29-30, where Jesus repeats the great statement of faith from the Old Testament, Deuteronomy 6:4-5: "Hear, O Israel: the Lord our God the Lord is one. You shall love the Lord your God with all your heart and with all your soul and with all your might."

Jesus confirms that this is a true statement. The seeker may still believe that you believe in three gods. The three gods he believes we worship are God, his female companion, Mary, and their son, Jesus. We must make it clear that to Christians this belief is blasphemy!

Remember the primary issues.

A fourth guideline for conversation is not to allow yourself to be diverted. Always remember what the primary issues really are. Depending on your Muslim friend's orientation, he or she may be either seeking eternal life, or seeking solutions for today's problems. Muslims tend to emphasize many other issues besides the eternal ones. They will talk to you about social, political, military, and economic issues. They will speak about the community of all Muslims and the solutions for man's problems that exist in Islam—for Islam is a total way of life. The eternal issues are the ones they may not want to address. These deal with forgiveness of sin, the human condition, and assurance of heaven.

Their felt needs represent the pain and uncertainty of everyday life. It is important to address these needs also—by pointing them to Jesus as the One who heals, delivers from oppression, and answers prayer. Pray with them and believe for a miracle. At such times, remember the words of Jesus in Mark 10:45: "For even the Son of Man came not to be served but to serve, and to give his life as a ransom for many." We come to serve people.

Make a positive statement of what you believe.

A fifth guideline to conversation is to make a positive statement of what you believe. We have just discussed how forces can work against getting to the primary issues. You don't always want to be responding to the Muslim's questions; also look for opportunities to share what you believe and why. In 1 Peter 3:15 (NIV) we are advised to "always be prepared to give an answer to everyone who asks you to give the reason for the hope that you have. But do this with gentleness and respect...."

Also explain how Jesus changed your life. You want the listener to understand that the Christian life is not just a different set of rules to live by, but that you are sharing about a relationship and a new life with Jesus. Offer Jesus as an experience, as a friend—not just a historical figure.

Give your personal testimony.

Again, we emphasize one of the best ways you can make a positive statement is to share your personal testimony. When you give your testimony of how you came to Christ, you convey a number of truths: First, you were not born a follower of Christ. Second, it was an event that happened to you. Third, you made a conscious decision to follow Jesus. There was a reason you made this decision. You were desperate for a change in your life. But in the end you did it because you had sinned and knew you needed a Savior.

In all this you are conveying another important message: you know God and have experienced His love and forgiveness—all because you have met Jesus personally. The verse that tells us this is John 17:3: "And this is eternal life, that they know you, the only true God, and Jesus Christ whom you have sent." As you speak about Jesus as the Savior who forgives sin, you will be proclaiming that you and all men are sinners. Remember, to the Muslim, man is basically good by nature and just needs to be reminded of Allah's laws. The Bible of course tells us that "all have sinned" (Romans 3:23) and the "wages of sin is death" (Romans 6:23). You could point out that 1 John 1:8-9 is written to Christians.

Be patient while God works.

The seventh guideline is that you must be patient while God works in the person's heart. For the Muslim to accept Jesus as Savior is very often a process that can take months or years. Your patience allows him the time to truly consider the cost of commitment. For his whole life he has been warned about Christians and the shame of his ever becoming one. Many of the key concepts of our faith are the exact opposite of what he has learned throughout his life.

In John 16:12 (NIV), Jesus tells the disciples, "I have much more to say to you, more than you can now bear."

Then He promises that when the Spirit comes, He will guide them into all truth. If that was the case with the disciples, how much more it is true for Muslim seekers. The disciples didn't understand it all—and they had been with Jesus for more than three years! We need patience because "some plant, some water, but God gives the increase" (author's paraphrase).

Touch the heart and not just the mind.

The eighth guideline is to remember to touch or make contact with both the mind and the heart, the seat of the emotions. We tend to judge a person's orthodoxy by what he knows and by certain statements of the faith that he can affirm. This is fine, but people are not saved and brought into the Kingdom by knowledge. Many wicked men in history have known the Scriptures well, but never surrendered to the person of Christ. The Muslim needs more than knowledge; he needs an experience of the heart, an emotional experience. He needs to encounter the love of God, His forgiveness, and His grace. Jesus knew this about His disciples for in John 15:9 He said to them, "As the Father has loved me, so have I loved you. Abide in my love." Jesus showed His love by making a great sacrifice. Muslims are people of emotion, and there is nothing wrong with appealing to those emotions, for both the mind and emotions influence the will, the part of man that must make the decision to follow Christ.

Give your friend the written Word of God.

In this final guideline for conversation, you stop talking and let the Holy Spirit speak. We suggest that you give your friend a copy of the Scriptures. In Hebrews 4:12, we are reminded that "the word of God is living and active, sharper than any two-edged sword, piercing to the division of soul and of spirit, of joints and of marrow, and discerning the thoughts and intentions of the heart." In the end, the Word of God is best able to answer the Muslim's questions under the guidance of the Holy Spirit. We have the promise that the Holy Spirit can guide people into all truth (John 16:13).

When you give this gift of a gospel portion or the entire New Testament, explain what it is and that it will bring blessing to them. (The Arabic word for blessing is *baraka*.) Wrap it in plain white paper and emphasize that it is a special gift for them from God. If you have marked your Bible, explain it is an aid to studying it and learning God's Word. We do not recommend giving Muslims a used Bible, especially one that has been written in. Pray with the person and ask God to make His Word a blessing to them. Let them hear you talk to God and remember a key to ministry is to be led by the Spirit of God.[10]

CONCLUSION

We should seek to find those who have an interest in spiritual realities. Just as in our own culture, there are Muslim people who are open to God and others who are not. Remember there are those who call themselves Muslims who are that in name only, but have no interest in spiritual truth. Ask God to help you to communicate in a way that will cause Muslims to look toward Jesus, their only hope.

Testimony

Khalida went through a crisis in which she became homeless, and ended up walking the streets. She went into a store. "The moment I entered the store," she says, "the woman storekeeper was very loving and very cheerful. She hugged me. I was kind of scared. Should I trust her? But I felt so drawn to the store. I said, 'I'm here looking for a job. I can cook and clean.' She said, 'I need someone to cook and clean for me.' We started having a relationship, which started getting deeper and deeper. When she found out I was homeless, she invited me into her home. She didn't even charge me rent. And then she helped me get a place of my own.

"Then she started telling me about her beliefs. She told me she is a Christian and that God has a Son. I told her, 'You guys are fools. Everybody needs to come to Islam. God is not weak that he needs a son to help him.' She said, 'It's okay to believe what you believe, but I would like to share what I believe.' ...

"I started to think, *Whatever this woman has, that's what I want. She has her faith, and it made her a very helpful person.* Every person that entered her store, she greeted with a smile. I didn't have love; I faked it. I felt lonely and unsatisfied. I was the opposite of that woman. After two years of hanging around with this woman, I wanted some of what she had."

Prayer Points:

- Pray that God will give you a sense of the lostness Muslims feel because they have no guidance.

- Pray for a genuine burden for Muslims.

- Pray that your Muslim friend would be willing to answer some of the suggested questions from this lesson.

Action Steps:

- Look back at the guidelines for conversation. Consider two items you will endeavor to use in your next encounter with your Muslim friend.

- Look back at the list of Muslim spiritual needs. Imagine your friend asking one of those questions. How would you answer from Scripture and your life experience?

Review Questions:

1. How can a Christian overcome the fear of reaching out to a Muslim?

2. What will be required on your part to establish a friendship with a Muslim?

3. From the list of **Do's**, what four do you consider most important and why?

4. From the list of **Do nots**, what four are most important and why?

5. How would you respond to the Muslim accusation that the Bible is no longer trustworthy—that it has been corrupted?

6. According to this lesson, what does it mean to touch the heart and not just the head?

NOTES

NOTES

NOTES

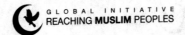

NOTES

DEVELOPING CHRISTIANS FROM A MUSLIM BACKGROUND (CMBS) (SPIRIT-LED OBEDIENCE)

The objective for Lesson 5 is:

That you would model the
"New Life" before Muslims.

CHAPTER SUMMARY

Jesus placed the focus of the Great Commission upon making disciples out of all nations. "Go therefore and make disciples of all nations, baptizing them in the name of the Father and of the Son and of the Holy Spirit, teaching them to observe all that I have commanded you. And behold, I am with you always, to the end of the age" (Matthew 28:19-20). The means of fulfilling the Great Commission includes going, baptizing, and teaching. But the goal of the Great Commission seems to be making disciples. Jesus placed the responsibility of making disciples upon His disciples. Similarly, He obliged new believers to be baptized and to observe all of His commands. Thus, Jesus defines discipleship as identification with the Father, Son, and Holy Spirit and as obedience to His teaching.

Testimony

N.K.: "The most important thing we do is speak the truth, the Word of God. Muslims have to hear it. It is more powerful than good deeds. A lot of things they disagree with in the Quran. They just need to hear the other side—the truth—the Word of God. They will distinguish it when they hear it."

CHAPTER OUTLINE

Replicating the Environment

    Introduction

    Muslim-Background-Specific Discipleship

The Disciple's New Guide

The Disciple's New Lord and Friend

Your New Life

Your New Helper, the Holy Spirit

Your New Community

Disciples of Christ Live Differently (Ephesians 5:1-5)

Your New Struggle

Our Enemies Are Not People!

A Personal Testimony from a Laborer

Conclusion

    Prayer Points

    Action Steps

    Review Questions

REPLICATING THE ENVIRONMENT

Introduction

Spiritual formation of new believers presents a challenge in the best of circumstances. When one considers the vast differences between Muslims and Christians, he or she realizes the magnified challenge. Islamic society seeks to isolate converts to Christianity from society, silence their witness, and pressure them to revert to Islam. Converts from Islam can face persecution and potential martyrdom. "It should be remembered that when Orthodox Muslims discuss the idea of 'religious freedom,' they mean that all others are free to become Muslims, but Muslims are not free to change their religion."[11]

Jesus commissioned the Church to make disciples out of all nations. Laborers in the harvest field are concerned with making disciples, but more specifically, making disciples out of converts from Islam. Of course this includes the physical transport of Christ's teachings across geographic and/or cultural boundaries, but it involves much more. If the evangelistic message must be packaged differently for various cultures, why then would Christians attempt the continued spiritual transformation of new believers without considering their cultural and religious backgrounds?

Muslim-Background-Specific Discipleship

Too many Muslim converts have reverted to Islam. The successful spiritual formation of converts from Islam requires bridge building from Islamic beliefs, values, and practices to Christian beliefs, values, and practices. Disciplers must teach the Word in such a way that clearly distinguishes sound biblical doctrine from ideologies and cultural practices in a society detrimental to true discipleship. Disciplers must also distinguish biblical truth from church culture that is not biblical.

THE DISCIPLE'S NEW GUIDE

The Bible is the disciple's new guide. "Your word is a lamp to my feet and a light to my path" (Psalm 119:105). The first chapter of the Quran is a prayer for guidance that Muslims pray to keep them on the right path. They believe this path leads to Allah's mercy, not to his judgment. They believe that they obtain guidance in Allah's revelation, the Quran. Muslims do not believe that they need redemption, but that they need guidance to keep them from stumbling. For them, the Quran reveals Allah's will and law, not his character. The Bible must be presented as God's self-revelation that guides people to right relationship with Him. While Muslims believe that the Quran was sent down in the same form that it exists in heaven, Christians believe that the Holy Spirit inspired writers and they communicated God's message. Christians further believe that as the Bible is the written Word of God, Jesus Christ is the Living Word of God.

As a new follower of Jesus, your disciple has put his or her faith in Christ to guide him or her on the right path. This does not mean that we now have a new list of do's and don'ts. What it does mean is that Jesus has paid the price for us to be acceptable in God's sight. The new path is not a path of law but a path of grace. God *did* give laws to His people to obey. But, He has also provided enough grace to enable His people to live according to His expectations. God has put us on the right path and now we trust Him to keep us on that path.

We believe that the Bible is the written Word of God. As God's Word, the Bible is our rule of faith and conduct. The Holy Spirit directed the authorship of Scripture. Inspiration means that God breathed His Holy Spirit into men and women so that they were moved to record His revelation without error. Even though the Bible was written over a period of 1,500 years by at least 40 authors from different backgrounds, it displays miraculous unity. As your disciples read Scripture, encourage them to look for words that are used to mean "God's message." Any references to Scripture, the law of the Lord, statutes, Word of God, decrees, commands, precepts, teachings, and so forth, should be understood as portions or the complete Bible. The Bible is revelation. God reveals himself and His law to humankind.

The Bible provides examples for instruction, gives wisdom, makes disciples, reveals truth, gives freedom, leads to salvation, teaches, reproves, corrects, trains, prophesies, predicts, shows how prophecy is fulfilled, gives hope, establishes, and makes disciples. In other words, Scripture produces disciples. It forms Christ in you (Galatians 4:19). Summed up, the Bible is our guide. Since the Bible conveys God's message, it carries the same authority as if God spoke to us personally. Therefore, it is important that disciples read God's message daily, study the Bible and commit as much of Scripture to memory as possible.

THE DISCIPLE'S NEW LORD AND FRIEND

We need to compare and show the contrasts between the God of the Bible and the Allah of the Quran. "'God is spirit, and those who worship him must worship in spirit and truth" (John 4:24). "For although there may be so-called gods in heaven or on earth—as indeed there are many 'gods' and many 'lords'— yet for us there is one God, the Father, from whom are all things and for whom we exist, and one Lord, Jesus Christ, through whom are all things and through whom we exist" (1 Corinthians 8:5-6).

As a follower of Jesus your disciples are gaining a new understanding of who God is and what He is like. God is a self-revealing God. The true God reveals himself in three persons: God the Father, God the Son, and God the Holy Spirit. Although the Bible neither uses nor explains the term Trinity, it teaches the concept.

Concerning mankind's relationship with God, Christians believe in *transcendence*, or distance. This means that God distances himself from creation, and is superior to creation. "As the heavens are higher than the earth, so are my ways higher than your ways and my thoughts than your thoughts" (Isaiah 55:9). Christians also believe in *immanence*, or nearness. This refers to God's presence in the world and His interaction with creation.

Not only does the Bible teach immanence, but it describes God as *love*. "Anyone who does not love does not know God, because God is love" (1 John 4:8). Paul refers to God as "the God of love and peace" (2 Corinthians 13:11). To whom does God demonstrate His benevolence? See Matthew 5:45; Psalm 145:16; John 3:16. God's love made us His children (1 John 3:1). In addition to transcendence, immanence, and love, God is:

- Holy
- Self-existent
- Just, Righteous
- Merciful
- Unchanging
- Omnipresent (present everywhere) and Omniscient (all knowing)
- Omnipotent (all powerful)

Jesus refers to himself as the believer's friend. Jesus calls us friends because He has shared with us the greatest revelation of the ages. Abraham was called the friend of God because of his faith (James 2:23). The fact that Jesus is your best friend does not mean that He deserves any less respect and honor.

The Son is the "radiance of God's glory" as the ray is the light of the sun (Hebrews 1:3, NIV). This verse says that Jesus is "the exact representation of his [God's] being." A mark is the exact impression of the seal. In Colossians 1:15, Paul says that Jesus Christ is the "image of the invisible God, the firstborn over all creation." Notice that "firstborn over all creation," in Colossians 1:15, does not mean that Jesus was the first one created. It means that as heir and like all firstborn sons, He has certain privileges, rights, and authority over creation. Jesus is not merely a reflection of deity; **He is the exact, authentic representation of God's essence.**

The process by which Jesus came to earth in the form of a human being is called the Incarnation. The author of Hebrews writes about the Incarnation, "Therefore he had to be made like his brothers in every respect" (Hebrews 2:17). "During the days of Jesus' life on earth, he offered up prayers and petitions with fervent cries and tears to the one who could save him from death, and he was heard because of his reverent submission" (Hebrews 5:7, NIV).

Christ humbled himself, becoming obedient to death—not just any death, but death on a cross. Death by crucifixion was for the worst criminals. It was degrading, humiliating, and excruciatingly painful. Jesus suffered immensely. As the pure and Holy Son of God, He left heaven, humbled himself, and became as nothing (Hebrews 2:7). As shown earlier, He did it to supply the sacrifice for the sins of humanity. God exalted Jesus because of His obedience (Philippians 2:6-11). This means that Jesus emptied himself of His prerogatives of deity. He did not cease being God. He voluntarily laid aside the use of His prerogatives as God (John 1:1-14). The best description of the Incarnation is found in verse 14: "The Word became flesh and dwelt among us."

Although the passage does not explain exactly how He accomplished it, the writer to the Hebrews mentions God's way for taking care of humanity's sin problem: The Son "provided purification for sins" (Hebrews 1:3, NIV). Christians believe that the vicarious atonement of Christ provided salvation from judgment, deliverance from the power of sin and death, and acceptance by God. Jesus understood it as His mission. **His sacrifice distinguishes Christianity from all other religions.** Jesus explained that all the Scriptures predicted His suffering. He said, "This is what is written: The Messiah will suffer and rise from the dead on the third day, and repentance for the forgiveness of sins will be preached in his name to all nations, beginning at Jerusalem" (Luke 24:46-47, NIV).

Moses (Deuteronomy 18:15) and all the prophets predicted the coming of one who would turn everyone from their wicked ways (Acts 3:22-26). When you read the entire context of Acts 3:17-21, it is clear who Peter believed that Moses was speaking of in Deuteronomy 18:15. He was the same one the prophets spoke of, the offspring of Abraham who would bless all peoples on earth, the one that God raised up from the dead, and the one who will wipe out the sins of the people and turn them from their wicked ways. Peter was specific. This one was the Christ (Messiah) and Lord (Acts 3:20).

Paul wrote and referred to the return of Jesus many times. He clearly tells the Thessalonians that the resurrection of the righteous dead will accompany the return of Christ. The resurrection and return of Christ have several other implications for believers to consider. Paul tells the Corinthians that at the last trumpet the dead will be raised imperishable and the living will be changed instantaneously (1 Corinthians 15:51-52). The Bible also teaches that the unrighteous will be resurrected (John 5:28-29). The idea of the second coming includes a great final judgment for the unrighteous in the future (Matthew 25:46).

YOUR NEW LIFE

"Therefore, if anyone is in Christ, he is a new creation. The old has passed away; behold, the new has come" (2 Corinthians 5:17). Since Muslims and Christians understand sin differently, we must articulate the biblical position on the sinful nature of humanity, explain the biblical path to salvation, and enumerate the benefits of salvation. This will begin a process helping the new believer have a disciplined life focused on Bible study, prayer, fellowship, ministry, and fruit bearing.

The apostle Paul echoed the Old Testament and the teaching of the New Testament when he said, "There is no one righteous, not even one" (Romans 3:10, NIV). Humankind's sinful nature (Galatians 5:17) has passed to all people because of Adam's sin. Everyone is born with this sinful nature and eventually yields to sin, thereby succumbing to that sinful nature. Jesus taught that sin comes from the heart (Matthew 15:18-19). Before people sin outwardly, they defile themselves with their own evil thoughts and intentions. Sin is more than committing wrong deeds. It is willful disobedience that comes from a sinful nature. Sin kills, and it separates people from God. Adam and Eve were expelled from the Garden of Eden, and from the presence of God. Sin erodes the image of God in people.

Salvation and righteousness in God's sight cannot be earned by attempting to do good deeds. God offers it freely as we believe on His Son. **Sin earns wages; God gives salvation.** Christians believe that sin has separated all humans from God. Each individual possesses responsibility and can do nothing to reinstate that fellowship on his or her own initiative. All deserve eternal punishment and banishment from the presence of God. Salvation refers to that act of God whereby He provides deliverance from the bondage, guilt, and penalty of sin. God provided salvation by offering Jesus as a sacrifice for the sins of the world. "Ransom" (Mark 10:45) means to purchase something back that once belonged to the purchaser. Adam and Eve lived in fellowship with God, but sin broke that fellowship.

John refers to Jesus as the Righteous One (1 John 2:1,

NIV). That is why John could say, "He is the atoning sacrifice for our sins, and not only for ours but also for the sins of the whole world" (1 John 2:2, NIV). Because of the death of His holy Son as a substitute for sinners, a righteous God can pardon a guilty race without compromise. One may ask, "But how does an individual appropriate salvation?"

The Holy Spirit convicts people of their sin, convinces them of the righteousness of Christ, and of the reality of judgment (John 16:8-11). What must the sinner do to be saved? Paul said that in order to be saved, the sinner must confess with his mouth that Jesus is Lord, and the sinner must believe in his heart that God raised Him from the dead (Romans 10:9-11).

The whole sin problem begins with unbelief. The path to salvation begins with believing. It is not a matter of works and deeds. It is a matter of faith. We can call Romans 10:9-11 the Christian confession of faith. In confessing Jesus as Lord, we are affirming to the Church and to the world that we will serve and obey Jesus. By saying that we believe in the resurrection, we are also saying that we believe in His atoning death. The Resurrection affirms the deity of Jesus: "and was declared to be the Son of God in power according to the spirit of holiness by his resurrection from the dead, Jesus Christ our Lord" (Romans 1:4). Furthermore, the Resurrection affirms the efficacy of His atoning death. "He was delivered over to death for our sins and was raised to life for our justification" (Romans 4:25, NIV). Peter told the crowd in Jerusalem that they must repent and be baptized (Acts 2:36-39). Repentance means the sinner confesses and forsakes sin. Repentance not only affects what we believe but also what we do.

The Holy Spirit changes the new believer by creating new life (John 3:3-8). God forgives sin and cancels the guilt and punishment (Romans 3:21-26; 8:1). Through Jesus, everyone who believes is justified. *Justification* is a legal term. Believers are declared innocent, and God views them as though they never sinned. What wonderful salvation Jesus provides for believers! How can a person be made righteous? Paul explains: God does it through faith in Christ.

God's salvation through Christ's sacrifice provides so much for the believer:

- The promised Holy Spirit (Acts 2:29-33)

- Forgiveness of sins and the gift of the Holy Spirit (Acts 2:38-39)

- No condemnation (Romans 8:1)

- Freedom from the law of sin (Romans 8:2)

- A destiny in heaven with Jesus (John 14:1-4)

- Eternal inheritance (Hebrews 9:15)

- Eternal life and security (John 10:27-28)

- The kingdom of God (John 3:1-3)

"I have been crucified with Christ. It is no longer I who live, but Christ who lives in me. And the life I now live in the flesh I live by faith in the Son of God, who loved me and gave himself for me" (Galatians 2:20).

A new life is that of a disciple. A disciple is a follower. As a follower of Jesus Christ we must model our lives after Him. He is our pattern and great example in all things. The disciple makes Christ the Lord of his or her life. A key verse for discipleship is: "And he said to all, 'If anyone would come after me, let him deny himself and take up his cross daily and follow me'" (Luke 9:23). Jesus places three demands on His disciples: (1) deny themselves, (2) take up their crosses daily, (3) follow Christ.

There must be a change in the life of the disciple. Holding on to the old life will kill spiritual life. The disciple will not grow spiritually, and he or she will die spiritually. Lifeless Christians do not produce fruit, do not contribute to ministry, do not contribute to the community life of the church, are poor witnesses of Christ, and they are in danger of reverting to their old lifestyle or religion.

The phrase "whoever loses his life for me" is found in all four Gospels and in two Gospels more than once. Jesus gives this saying great emphasis. The culture of the kingdom of God is different from the world's culture. The standards, motives, goals, and lifestyles of the followers of Christ are counterculture to the world. Standing up against the world's ways is not popular. But Jesus promises the disciple will find new life in following Him. The life Jesus gives is full of joy, purpose, and satisfaction.

Some of those who were listening to Christ that day witnessed the coming of the kingdom of God (Luke 9:27). It was not ushered in militarily, but by the death of Christ upon the cross. Crosses are made to die upon, not display. Jesus wants His disciples to deny themselves, pick up their crosses, follow Him, and die. This means that a disciple must die to self and former lifestyles—and even be willing to die literally if necessary.

Prayer is one of the disciplines of cross bearing. We are not talking about prescribed rituals, dry routines, vain repetitions, or meaningless forms. We are talking about conversing with a heavenly Father. God hears our prayers and He speaks to us. Old Testament life and theology placed heavy emphasis on prayer. John taught his disciples to pray (Luke 11:1). Jesus had set an example before His disciples as He prayed regularly. One day His disciples came to Him while He was praying. They did not ask Him to teach them how to preach powerfully, how to evangelize persuasively, how to interpret Scripture exactly, nor did they ask for enhancement of any other ministerial gift. In Luke 11:1, one of His disciples said, "Lord, teach us to pray." This was certainly an appropriate request because Jesus prayed often, emphasizing the importance of prayer by deed.

YOUR NEW HELPER, THE HOLY SPIRIT

"'I will ask the Father, and He will give you another Helper, that He may be with you forever'" (John 14:16, NASB). "'But you will receive power when the Holy Spirit comes on you; and you will be my witnesses in Jerusalem, and in all Judea and Samaria, and to the ends of the earth'" (Acts 1:8, NIV). The same Spirit who empowered individuals in the Old Testament, anointed Jesus, and emboldened the early believers, helps disciples today. He empowers believers for service, exalts Christ, and teaches believers about Jesus.

The same Holy Spirit who empowered Jesus Christ is available to help believers today. Jesus said that He would not leave us alone, but would send another "Helper" (John 14:16, NASB), and He promised that the Helper would be with us forever. Jesus then identifies the Helper as the Holy Spirit (John 14:26). In the same way that the Spirit helped Jesus in ministry, He helped the apostles and believers in the Early Church to fulfill the Church's mission. John identified Jesus as the Christ, the Lamb of God who takes away the sin of the world, the Son of God, the one who would carry out judgment, and the one who would baptize with the Holy Spirit (Mark 1:7-8; Luke 3:15-17; John 1:29-34). Jesus told His disciples that the gospel would be preached in His name to all nations, He would send His Father's promise, and that the Spirit would empower them (Luke 24:47-49).

The promised Holy Spirit is available to everyone who believes and repents of his or her sinful nature. When a person repents and believes, that individual is born of the Spirit (John 3:3-8). The moment we repent and believe that Jesus is the Son of God, that He died for our sins and that God raised

Jesus from the dead, then the Holy Spirit dwells in us! We call this regeneration.

What happened on Pentecost supplied the disciples with power to witness about the gospel. Jesus had returned to the Father and was now baptizing believers in the Holy Spirit. As the Spirit had empowered Old Testament saints for special ministries, and as the Spirit had empowered Jesus Christ for ministry, now the Spirit would make a difference in the lives of the apostles and believers in the Early Church. Pentecostals believe that the Spirit's work in regeneration and the baptism in the Holy Spirit are two separate experiences. They may at times seem to occur simultaneously (Acts 10:44-46), and at other times there may be a time interval between the experiences (Acts 19:1-7). It is more important to notice that there is a distinctive difference in the purpose of the two separate experiences. *Regeneration* creates new life in the believer. He or she becomes alive to the Spirit, and God lives in the believer by the Spirit. The believer begins to grow in his or her new life. *The baptism* in the Holy Spirit supplies the new believer with power for service.

Read Acts 5:17-42. The power and joy that the Holy Spirit supplied in the lives of the believers in Jerusalem could not be silenced by persecution or threats. Perhaps your friend who converted from Islam has been persecuted or threatened for their faith in Jesus Christ. They need the power of the Holy Spirit to help them. Laborers among Muslims have documented the necessity of the baptism in the Holy Spirit for converts from Islam. Converts often face persecution, isolation, and physical danger. Those who have not received God's available power through the baptism in the Holy Spirit have often reverted to Islam because of extreme pressure. The Spirit helps people just as He helped believers in the Book of Acts.

Persecution broke out against the church in Jerusalem (Acts 8:1). The believers, except for the apostles, were scattered throughout Judea and Samaria. Philip preached the Word in Samaria and many believed and were baptized. The apostles in Jerusalem sent Peter and John to them, and when they arrived they prayed for them to receive the Holy Spirit. By this time the apostles felt that it was necessary for all believers to receive the same experience that they had received on the Day of Pentecost. In Acts 2:1-4, all were filled with the Holy Spirit and began to speak in tongues. The Holy Spirit came on all who heard the message in Acts 10:44-46; 11:15-16. Peter and the others knew that the Holy Spirit had come upon them because they heard the Gentiles speaking in tongues just as the Spirit had come on them in the beginning. Paul laid his hands on the disciples after they were baptized in water (Acts 19:1-7). The Spirit came on them, and they spoke in tongues and prophesied. What occurred in all three instances where people were baptized in the Holy Spirit? They all spoke in tongues.

In Acts 8:15-17, Peter and John prayed and laid hands on the disciples in Samaria, and they received the Holy Spirit. There is no mention that they spoke in tongues. But something visible did occur. It was so demonstrative that Simon attempted to purchase the ability to dispense the Holy Spirit. The passage does not describe what that was, but from the other three instances it seems obvious.

YOUR NEW COMMUNITY

"... God's household, which is the church of the living God, the pillar and foundation of the truth" (1 Timothy 3:15, NIV). "To him be glory in the church and in Christ Jesus throughout all generations, for ever and ever! Amen" (Ephesians 3:21, NIV).

Islam provides community for Muslims. When a Muslim becomes a follower of Christ, that community ostracizes him or her, and former social and economic associations cease. The Church becomes the disciple's new family and community. Paul's metaphors for the Church address the Church's nature and its obligation to believers as well as non-believers. Membership in the new community has privileges as well as responsibilities.

The New Testament gives instructions for disciples living in community and in the world. For Christians, living in community means relating to other believers as members of the Church. The Church includes all born-again believers who have been placed into the body of Christ by the Spirit of God (1 Corinthians 12:13). The term *church* is used to refer to individual groups of believers (Galatians 1:2; Colossians 4:15), and to the universal Church (Colossians 1:18; Ephesians 1:22-23).

Jesus said to Peter, "I will build my church, and the gates of Hades will not overcome it" (Matthew 16:18, NIV). In the Great Commission, Jesus told the eleven to "make disciples of all nations" (Matthew 28:19). He did not mention church planting in the Great Commission. Somehow, the apostles knew that their task would be to evangelize, make disciples out of the converts, and group these converts into communities of believers called churches. Thus, the primary ministry of the apostles was making disciples and planting churches. Although Jesus initiated His Church, the apostles—especially Paul—through the power of the Holy Spirit, articulated what the Church should be.

Paul uses metaphors to describe the Church and to describe the disciples who make up the Church. "Consequently, you are no longer foreigners and strangers, but fellow citizens with God's people" (Ephesians 2:19, NIV). Citizenship indicates rights and obligations. As part of the church there are certain blessings and responsibilities. As converts participate in a local church, they will be ministered to, but they should also mature to the point where they are making a contribution to the overall ministry of the church. **Some Christians have never learned that they have a responsibility to minister to others.**

Paul also uses the metaphor of the household or family in 2:19. (He also uses it elsewhere in his letters to refer to the Church.) The word *household* has often been referred to as immediate or extended family. However, in God's family, there are no cousins; all are sons and daughters, brothers and sisters. Family membership suggests greater intimacy and greater responsibility than citizenship does. Family members love and care for one another. In the household, babies are nurtured, children are educated and at times disciplined, mature adults assume responsibilities for the welfare of the family, and the sick and elderly are cared for. This is all done in an atmosphere of love and acceptance. The idea of membership indicates equal partnership, and membership has rights. Joy and sorrow are shared. Family members are helped, encouraged, and depended upon. Birth, baptism, graduation, marriage, raising a family, and death sometimes all take place within the context of one local congregation. Sometimes because of relocation, a disciple has the privilege of being part of two or more local church families in his or her lifetime. Experiences, both sad and joyous, are shared, as are religious holidays.

Paul's favorite metaphor for the Church is the "body of Christ." Christ ministered through His physical body on earth; now His body is the Church. It was common imagery in the ancient world to speak of individuals who were part of a larger group and drawn together for a common purpose, as members, and the group as a body. Perhaps the image was made real to Paul on the road to Damascus, when he heard Jesus say, "Saul, Saul, why do you persecute me?" (Acts 9:4, NIV).

The image of the body of Christ demonstrates relationships as they should be between individuals in the church. *Christians never live individually in relationship to the Lord without regard for others.* In 1 Corinthians 12:12-27, Paul develops the concept of interdependence among the members of the body. The metaphor of the human body teaches that the body is one complete unit only as all of its functioning members are healthy and in place. In the body of Christ, each member is an integral part of the whole. Members are formed into one body by their common experience in the Spirit.

The body is one, but made up of parts. Each part has a unique function, and all parts need one another. "God has combined the members of the body" and there should be no division in the body. Parts, or members, should have equal concern for each other. The parts of the body share suffering and rejoicing. The body of Christ is the most wonderful community when it is functioning properly. The body in Corinth was not functioning properly, and Paul wrote the letter to correct them. The New Testament continually instructs believers to demonstrate Christ's love. Jesus commanded His disciples to love one another (John 13:34-35), and He said that love for one another is the evidence of true discipleship.

Paul uses the metaphor of the temple to instruct the Corinthians concerning their common experience with the Spirit (1 Corinthians 3:16-17). The imagery pictures the Holy Spirit living collectively in all the believers and in each disciple individually. Paul addresses division in the church in Corinth. They are building God's temple in Corinth. The Church is not to be destroyed by divisions, controversies, or other sins because it is the temple of the Holy Spirit. God will destroy anyone who does anything to damage the temple, the local church. This metaphor teaches disciples what their attitude should be toward the Church and how they should treat individual members and the body as a whole.

The Church exists to edify the saints and equip them for ministry. In this regard, the Church's mission is to form Christ in each believer. Jesus himself gave gifts to the Church: apostles, prophets, evangelists, pastors and teachers (Ephesians 4:7-13). The purpose of these gifts is to prepare disciples to do "works of service," of ministry, in order to edify the body of Christ. The ultimate goal is that all disciples reach maturity, becoming like Christ.

Jesus intended the Church to be the agency for evangelizing the world (Matthew 28:19-20). It appears that Jesus gave the Great Commission more than once. The account in Matthew emphasizes the making of disciples; this is discipleship. Mark's account emphasizes going and preaching to the whole world; this is world missions. Luke's account emphasizes the preaching of repentance and forgiveness of sins; this is evangelism. John's account emphasizes the sender; this is authority. The Book of Acts emphasizes empowerment for witnessing.

The program for evangelizing the world is the responsibility of every church member. All should support missions and ministries of the church with their prayers and finances. Not all members will be pastors, evangelists, or missionaries. But every disciple should be involved in ministry of some kind, and every disciple should be attempting to bring family and friends to Jesus.

The community of Christ's disciples lives in the world among unbelievers. One of the responsibilities of all church members is to live as witnesses in the world. God expected the Old Testament saints to be holy because they represented a holy God to the nations (Exodus 19:4-6; Leviticus 11:45). The Lord wanted His people to be free from the sins of surrounding nations, not contaminating themselves by taking wives from neighboring peoples (Ezra 9:1-10:44). The writers of the Old Testament constantly warned Israel concerning idolatry. The Old Testament protested false religion and evil culture while presenting high standards. The Ten Commandments declared unprecedented ideals.

The sacrificial system provided atonement for sin while teaching consecration to God and separation from the defilements of the world. Paul makes it clear that believers' lives should mirror their standing. "Since we have these promises, dear friends, let us purify ourselves from everything that contaminates body and spirit, perfecting holiness out of reverence for God" (2 Corinthians 7:1, NIV). Paul says that disciples should live by the Spirit (see Galatians 5:18). And then they will not live to gratify the desires of the sinful nature, or the flesh. True disciples strive to exemplify Christ's holy character. Paul addresses issues such as Christian concern for one another (1 Corinthians 12:12-26; Ephesians 4:32), attitudes (Ephesians 4:29-31) and morality (1 Corinthians 5:1-5). He said that God wants disciples to avoid sexual immorality (1 Thessalonians 4:3-6). "For God did not call us to be impure, but to live a holy life" (1 Thessalonians 4:7, NIV).

DISCIPLES OF CHRIST LIVE DIFFERENTLY (EPHESIANS 5:1-5)

Jesus said that His disciples should not limit their concern to Christians. Disciples of Christ love their enemies and pray for their persecutors; otherwise they are no better than the tax collectors and pagans (Matthew 5:43-47). This kind of love reflects God's selfless love (Matthew 6:48). This kind of love defies human logic. Human nature wants revenge against enemies. This is the way of the world, the way of Satan. Jesus wants His disciples to be different. Solomon stated the principle in the Old Testament. "If your enemy is hungry, give him food to eat; if he is thirsty, give him water to drink" (Proverbs 25:21, NIV). John the Baptist preached benevolence (Luke 3:11). Jesus said, "Give to the one who asks you, and do not turn away from the one who wants to borrow from you" (Matthew 5:42). Paul exhorted believers in Rome to help the needy and practice hospitality (Romans 12:13).

Benevolence includes helping and doing good to all people, but especially those who belong to the family of believers (Galatians 6:10). Furthermore, they should do good to others (Hebrews 13:16).

An important part of living in community for disciples of Christ is corporate worship. The Old Testament gives the model as it describes public worship in a number of passages. "Jehoshaphat bowed down with his face to the ground, and all the people of Judah and Jerusalem fell down in worship before the LORD" (2 Chronicles 20:18, NIV). The New Testament does not require certain postures for prayer or worship. It seems variety is encouraged. At times it is appropriate to bow down in reverence to an all-powerful, holy, and majestic God. "And when he had said these things, he knelt down and prayed with them all" (Acts 20:36). The Old Testament describes other forms of worship. "The whole assembly bowed in worship, while the musicians played and the trumpets sounded" (2 Chronicles 29:28, NIV). Psalms repeatedly calls the people to corporate worship.

Christians believe that Christ instituted certain rites which serve as visible signs of God's saving grace. Many call these rites "ordinances," since Christ ordered them to be observed. Baptism by immersion is commanded in the Scriptures. All who repent and believe on Christ as Savior and Lord are to be baptized. These disciples declare to the Church and to the world that they have died with Christ and that they have also been raised with Him to walk in newness of life.

Christians recognize Holy Communion, or the Lord's Supper, as a commemoration of Christ's suffering and death. Christians believe that Jesus established the Lord's Supper (1 Corinthians 11:23-27). Most recognize the necessity to repeat the ceremony regularly. The Lord's Supper symbolizes the fellowship that believers have with the Lord and with one another. All Christians who partake of the Lord's Supper should recognize the value of participating. It provides a means of grace and opportunity for spiritual growth. The symbols express our sharing of the divine nature of our Lord Jesus Christ (2 Peter 1:4), memorialize His suffering and death, and prophesy His second coming (1 Corinthians 11:26).

The Holy Spirit gives gifts for the fellowship, life, and ministry of the church. The apostle Paul explains that diversity, not uniformity, characterizes a healthy church, and he stresses the need for diversity within unity (1 Corinthians 12:4-31). In 1 Corinthians 13, Paul teaches believers to exercise gifts with love and concern for all members of the body. The individual who speaks in tongues speaks to God (14:2). His spirit is edified, but without interpretation the group receives no benefit. Since speaking in tongues accompanies the baptism in the Holy Spirit, believers in Corinth found it easy to exercise the gift of tongues by faith in the congregation, neglecting other gifts and thereby neglecting the needs of other members. The Spirit gives gifts for the edification of the entire church. When the Spirit edifies the body He edifies each and every member. Likewise, as the Spirit ministers to members individually, the whole body is edified.

Spiritual gifts provide supernatural enablement for believers to minister not only to the body of Christ, but to unbelievers also. The Spirit's ministry to unbelievers mainly has to do with convincing and convicting. The Spirit will convict the world of sin, that is, of unbelief. He will convince sinners of the righteousness that is only found in Jesus Christ and convince the world of certain judgment (John 16:8-11).

YOUR NEW STRUGGLE

Spiritual warfare! "For we do not wrestle against flesh and blood, but against the rulers, against the authorities, against the cosmic powers over this present darkness, against the spiritual forces of evil in the heavenly places" (Ephesians

6:12). Although it has been interpreted variously, the basic Islamic understanding of *jihad* refers to a Muslim's individual struggle against evil. This study puts that struggle into a Christian context. The study first identifies the enemy, who is not flesh and blood, but is the devil. Although Muslims attempt many methods of achieving spiritual power in order to overcome evil powers, the disciple learns that only Jesus possesses true authority over the enemy, and Jesus freely gives that authority to His disciples.

The enemy was first introduced in Genesis 3 as a serpent. John identifies the great dragon as the serpent of Genesis 3, and if there were any doubts, he clearly identifies him as Satan, the devil (Revelation 12:9; 20:2). The devil persuaded Adam and Eve to doubt God, disobey His Word, and sin. According to John, the devil is the one who leads the whole world astray (Revelation 12:9).

Christianity is not a system of this world. The world's religions are hostile toward the gospel of Jesus Christ. Whether they are steeped in law and have their adherents in bondage to a worldly system, or are full of demonic activity and have their followers in bondage to dark powers, these religions are anti-Christ. Often people who follow them do not coexist peacefully with followers of Jesus. Since Islam rejects the deity, lordship, and saving work of Jesus, a Muslim who wants to dedicate his or her life to Christ must overcome the *shahada covenant* he or she was born into. The shahada covenant identifies Muhammad as God's messenger, and hence the guide for all Muslims. Those discipling Muslims should discern the readiness of the new convert to pray for the breaking of the covenant of Muhammad—through the power of the Cross and blood of Jesus Christ, in His name.

Millions of people live in fear of evil spirits, blaming their circumstances on external forces beyond their control. Some attribute the incidental inconveniences of everyday life to the spirits, while others blame demons for disease, famine, war, and death. They feel helpless and powerless without the help of someone, something, or some place that has perceived power to counteract the effect of evil forces. Multitudes of people turn to magic, witchcraft, and other ways of manipulating the spirit world. These folks are more concerned with the answers to the problems of everyday life than with questions concerning God, eternity, and judgment.

The Holy Scripture presents the reality of the spirit world and the operation of spirit beings in the earthly realm. The New Testament records that God's choice servant, Jesus, dealt with evil spirits more than once. On one occasion, He encountered an evil spirit in an individual in a house of prayer in Capernaum and ordered the spirit to come out of the man. The evil spirit shook the man violently and came out of him with a shriek. The people were amazed that He taught with such authority and that even the evil spirits obeyed Him (Mark 1:23-27).

Although Satan is a powerful being, and though humans are no match for him, Jesus' victory over the devil gives His disciples authority and power over the works of the devil now. Followers of Christ do not have to live under Satan's bondage or in fear of his power. Disciples do not use superstition, witchcraft, or sorcery to engage the forces of the devil. Jesus said, "Whoever listens to you listens to me; whoever rejects you rejects me; but whoever rejects me rejects him who sent me" (Luke 10:16, NIV).

Jesus has given His disciples authority to drive out evil spirits and heal every disease and sickness (Matthew 10:1; Luke 10:19). Scripture arms disciples with an arsenal of spiritual weapons to help them in their struggle against the enemy (Ephesians 6:10-18). Paul begins by encouraging the Ephesians to be strong in the Lord and His mighty power. By this he reminds disciples that they do not have to rely on their own resources to combat the forces of hell. Paul reminds disciples that there is spiritual armor to help them stand against the devil's attacks. And then he informs them that the struggle is not against flesh and blood.

OUR ENEMIES ARE NOT PEOPLE!

God loves all people.

Some have identified "truth" (Ephesians 6:14) as the Word of God. In the same context Paul uses another metaphor to describe the Word of God in 6:17, and he leaves no room for misunderstanding. He states that the sword of the Spirit is the Word of God. So it seems unlikely that he would mix metaphors in the context while he is listing parts of the armor. While the Word is the source of truth, this is not the primary implication in 6:14. It may include the idea of the Word, or the Bible, but truth speaks of character and integrity. Disciples need integrity of character in order to stand. All spiritual weapons and gifts hang on one's character as all parts of a warrior's armor are buckled together by this belt. If the belt of truth is not buckled, no part of the armor will be available.

The "breastplate of righteousness" (6:14) primarily speaks of the righteousness of Christ. Revelation 12:10 says that Satan is the "accuser of our brothers." The devil cannot accuse disciples because Christ is the disciple's righteousness. When God looks at the disciple He does not see human weaknesses and sinful nature, He sees the righteousness of Christ. Although self-righteousness is as filthy rags (Isaiah 64:6), the disciple's heart and conscience should be clear, and his or her life should reflect Christ's holy character. The breastplate of "righteousness" is to be in "place."

Although runners usually ran barefoot, the soldier required combat boots to support and protect his feet. Is it strange that Paul uses the metaphor of soldiers' combat boots to refer to the gospel of peace? No. Disciples struggle with the enemy in bringing the gospel of peace to a troubled world. Actually, these combat boots are referred to as "readiness that comes from the gospel of peace" (6:15, NIV).

The "shield of faith" will "extinguish all the flaming arrows of the evil one" (6:16, NIV). The Roman soldier's shield was covered with leather and could be soaked in water, and it was capable of putting out flame tipped arrows. Satan will attempt to make disciples doubt, but these "fiery arrows" are extinguished by nothing else but faith. Against all odds, "Abraham believed God, and it was credited to him as righteousness" (Romans 4:3).

Our faith is not detached from our intellect. Paul tells the Ephesians to take the "helmet of salvation" (6:17). The decision to follow Christ is a conscious decision and an act of volition or will. "Therefore, I urge you, brothers and sisters, in view of God's mercy, to offer your bodies as a living sacrifice, holy and pleasing to God—this is your true and proper worship. Do not conform to the pattern of this world, but be transformed by the renewing of your mind. Then you will be able to test and approve what God's will is—his good, pleasing and perfect will" (Romans 12:1-2, NIV).

Furthermore, disciples need to guard what they allow to enter their minds. They need the helmet of salvation to protect their thought processes from destructive ideas. Disciples of Christ should be discrete as to what they view, read, or listen to. They have been saved and delivered from such deeds. It has often been stated that the "sword of the Spirit" (6:17) is the only offensive weapon in the soldier's arsenal of armor. Nothing is more effective against the enemy than the Word of God and prayer. Disciples who neglect these disciplines in their lives are not effective in their struggle against evil. God wants Christians to be victorious, not defeated! That is why Paul makes it clear that wearing the armor of God is not optional; it's required!

After listing the spiritual armor, Paul gives further direction. First, he urges the disciples in Ephesus to "pray in the Spirit on all occasions with all kinds of prayers and requests" (6:18, NIV). Paul uses the terminology "pray in the Spirit" as praying "in a tongue" (1 Corinthians 14:14-15). Praying in tongues edifies one's own spirit (1 Corinthians 14:4). While this is not the goal of public worship, self-edification strengthens believers in the struggle against the enemy. Perhaps this is why Paul said, "I thank God that I speak in tongues more than all of you" (1 Corinthians 14:18). **Disciples should pray every day.** Paul told the Ephesians that when they pray in the Spirit they should pray all kinds of prayers and make requests (6:18). This is one reason why it is important to be baptized in the Holy Spirit. You may not be used by the Spirit in the gift of tongues in the public worship service, but every disciple can become a spiritual giant, a warrior in the struggle against the forces of evil. Pray in the Spirit every day!

Jude echoes Paul's advice. "But you, beloved, building yourselves up in your most holy faith and praying in the Holy Spirit" (Jude 1:20). This translation shows that the way to build yourselves up on your most holy faith is by praying in the Spirit. It is important! Paul told the Romans that there are times when we do not know what we ought to pray for, but the Spirit intercedes for us (Romans 8:26). Disciples need to pray in the Spirit in order to succeed in their struggle against the forces of evil.

Many Christians, including Pentecostals, believe that the Atonement provides healing for our physical bodies. "Surely he has borne our griefs and carried our sorrows; yet we esteemed him stricken, smitten by God, and afflicted. But he was pierced for our transgressions; he was crushed for our iniquities; upon him was the chastisement that brought us peace, and with his wounds we are healed" (Isaiah 53:4-5). James gives the church instructions if someone is sick. "Is anyone among you sick? Let him call for the elders of the church, and let them pray over him, anointing him with oil in the name of the Lord. And the prayer of faith will save the one who is sick, and the Lord will raise him up. And if he has committed sins, he will be forgiven" (James 5:14-15).

Quick review:

- The devil is the disciple's enemy.

- The systems of this world are anti-Christ.

- Jesus has given His disciples authority and power over Satan and the forces of evil.

- Spiritual armor helps us in our struggle against evil.

- Praying in the Spirit is an effective and powerful method of praying.

- Healing for our physical bodies is provided in the Atonement.

A PERSONAL TESTIMONY FROM A LABORER

As a Muslim-background Christian, I am thankful that you have taken the time to read this book. I grew up as a Muslim in the United States, yet I never had the experience of someone sharing the gospel with me or inviting me to church or to youth group events. I believe the material in this book will assist you in sparing other Muslims my experience. My story had a happy ending as I read the Bible as a college student, and discovered who Jesus really is—not merely a prophet, but Lord, God and Savior.

I am confident this material has equipped you to reach out to my Muslim friends, family, and neighbors—and, by extension, to all Muslims who are living in our country. Hopefully, we have cut through the fog of fear, stigmas, and stereotypes. When I think of ministry to Muslims, my first thought is: *Let's have fun*. It's great interacting with people who typically love to discuss faith issues, are hospitable, and represent intriguing and interesting cultures and customs. And thanks also for praying for Muslim people, for that is what is opening hearts and doors in the Muslim world.

I believe Muslims need "discipleship from the first handshake." In church circles, we often compartmentalize evangelism and discipleship. Yet, since Muslims often delay making their true feelings and beliefs known, we should not be discouraged if it does not look like our Muslim friend is responding to our loving words and actions. Muslims are looking for spiritual mentors in trusting relationships. May the Holy Spirit empower us to fulfill this role.

Prayer Points:

- Pray that your new Christian friends will immerse themselves in the Word of God.

- Pray that the Lord will sustain them and help them as they "flesh out" their new life.

- Pray for them to be baptized with the Holy Spirit.

- Pray that the Christian community will model and assist in the convert's growth.

Action Steps:

- Consider the familiarity or lack thereof with the English language and provide the Bible in a format that will assist in discipleship.

- Make yourself easily/more available to mentor the new believer.

- Get the convert involved in the "believing" community.

Review Questions:

1. Why is it so difficult for Muslims to become true Bible-believing Christians?

2. Why is it difficult for Muslims to pray, "Our Father"?

3. Why is it important for Muslim people to understand the teaching about the Holy Spirit?

4. Why is it important for members of a local church to provide community for Christians from Islamic background?

5. How will a Muslim be expected to live differently once he or she becomes a follower of Jesus?

NOTES

NOTES

NOTES

NOTES

ENDNOTES

1. Larry A. Poston and Carl F. Ellis, Jr., *The Changing Face of Islam in America* (Camp Hill, PA: Horizon Books, 2000), p. 146

2. *Christianity Today*, April 3, 2000, p. 53

3. Tim Warner, Syllabus for Class in "Power Encounter" (Deerfield, IL: Trinity Evangelical Divinity School, 1998)

4. Sobhi Malek, "Islam Encountering Gospel Power" in M.A. Dempster, B.D. Klaus and D. Petersen, eds., *Called and Empowered: Global Mission in Pentecostal Perspective* (Peabody, MA: Henderson Publishers, 1991)

5. *Christianity Today*, April 3, 2000, p. 53

6. Colin Chapman, *Cross and Crescent* (Leicester, England: Inter-Varsity Press, 1995), p. 15

7. Ibid.

8. Poston and Ellis, p.159

9. David Armstrong, *Bible Conversations: Catholic-Protestant Dialogues on the Bible, Tradition and Salvation* (E-Book, 2007)

10. Anne Cooper, *Ishmael My Brother* (Grand Rapids: Monarch Books, 1993), p. 49

11. Don McCurry, *Healing the Broken Family of Abraham: New Life for Muslims* (Colorado Springs: Ministries to Muslims, 2001), p. 294

ADDENDUM

Regularly, people ask, "How can I pray for Muslims?" Here are three practical thoughts:

- FIND out more about Muslims in your area and throughout the world. Gather a group of believers who will commit to pray for their needs.

- FORM a data-gathering team. Ask team members to visit Muslims in your area. Access sites like www.GlobalInitiativeInfo.com, www.JumaaPrayer.org and www.JoshuaProject.com for information about praying for Muslims, especially for Muslim Unreached People Groups.

- FACILITATE the beginning of Jumaa Prayer Fellowships among your praying friends. Ideally, Global Initiative encourages believers to pray an hour on the Muslim holy day of Friday (Jumaa in Arabic) and to fast the Friday noon meal, if possible.

Last, consider three further things that will assist in praying for Muslims:

- SIMPLIFY. Don't make it overly complicated. In the beginning, simply implore the Lord to "reveal himself to Muslim peoples." He may do that through sending a messenger, providing a vision, extending the gift of healing, or in some other supernatural way.

- SUBSCRIBE. If you are not already a subscriber to the free magazine *Intercede*, request to be placed on the mailing list. Intercede will inform you in a structured way about prayer needs in the Muslim world.

- SIGN UP. Please visit www.Facebook.com/JumaaPrayer, www.JumaaPrayer.org, or Twitter @JumaaPrayer and indicate your intention to become a part of Jumaa Prayer Fellowship. We also have the Jumaa Prayer Fellowship App to keep you informed when you are on the go.

Join thousands of believers around the world who fast and pray on Fridays for Muslims. Prayer is not only the beginning, but it is the key to reaching Muslims, and we ask you to be an integral part.

PRAYER STRATEGIES FOR
MUSLIM PEOPLE

- Thank God and praise Him for the privilege of cooperating with Him through prayer in changing Muslim nations.

- Ask the Lord to call people who are willing to reach out and share the love of Christ with Muslims.

- Ask the Holy Spirit to open the hearts of Muslims toward the true Christian believers so that they will be receptive to the gospel.

- Pray that the Lord Jesus will continue to reveal himself to Muslims through dreams and visions.

- Ask the Lord to raise up strong local churches in the midst of Muslim people groups.

- Pray against spiritual forces that are hindering from engaging Muslims with faith.

CONTRIBUTING AUTHORS

Dr. Jim Bennett and his wife, Theda, began their missions ministry in Jordan in 1974. Over the past 43 years, Jim has served in numerous ministry positions, including: pastor, Seminary President, and Director of Center for Ministry to Muslims/Global Initiative: Reaching Muslim Peoples (GI). Currently, Jim is Director of Ministries at GI. Bennett holds a Doctor of Missiology from Trinity Evangelical Divinity School in Chicago.

Dr. Fred Farrokh is an Iranian-American with a Muslim family background, who met Jesus Christ as Savior in 1983. Fred and his wife, Annette, began full-time missions work among Muslims in 1998. Currently, Fred is an International Trainer with Global Initiative: Reaching Muslim Peoples. Farrokh holds a Ph.D. in Intercultural Studies from Assemblies of God Theological Seminary in Springfield, Missouri.

Dr. Ken Ferguson and his wife, Kathy, received their missionary appointment to the Middle East in 1980. In the years that followed, Ken served as pastor, college and seminary faculty, and in administration. Currently, Ken is an Associate Director of Training at Global Initiative: Reaching Muslim Peoples. Ferguson holds a Doctor of Ministry from Assemblies of God Theological Seminary.

Dr. Tommy Hodum and his wife, Sandy, are appointed missionaries with Assemblies of God U.S. Missions since 1984. In 1997, Tommy was named the national representative to Muslims with the Assemblies of God. Currently, Tommy serves as the U.S. Representative at Global Initiative: Reaching Muslim Peoples. Hodum holds a Doctor of Education from the University of Missouri.

Harry Morin and his wife, Vera, received appointment as Assemblies of God missionaries to Bangladesh in 1975. Beginning in 1994, Harry served Global Initiative: Reaching Muslim Peoples as an International Trainer. Harry has authored numerous booklets and articles on ministering to Muslims. Currently, Harry and Vera are enjoying the "retired" status.

Dr. Paul Parks is an appointed missionary with Assemblies of God World Missions since 1977. Although he started in Northern Africa, he and his family later worked in Jordan and Israel. Currently, Paul is an Associate Director of Training at Global Initiative: Reaching Muslim Peoples. Parks holds a Doctor of Ministry from Oral Roberts University in Tulsa.

ORDERING INFORMATION

GLOBAL INITIATIVE
REACHING **MUSLIM** PEOPLES
P.O. BOX 2730
SPRINGFIELD, MO 65801-2730
PH 417.866.3313 FX 417.866.3733
www.REACHINGMUSLIMPEOPLES.com
www.JUMAAPRAYER.org